STOCK MARKET INVESTING FOR TEENS MADE EASY

IN 5 STEPS YOU WILL DISCOVER THE SECRET PATH
TO BECOMING A MILLIONAIRE INVESTOR. THE
ULTIMATE TEENAGERS GUIDE TO MAKING MONEY
AND UNCOVERING RICHES.

THE YOUNG INVESTOR STOCK MARKET SERIES
BOOK ONE

THE YOUNG INVESTOR

THE YOUNG INVESTOR

QR CODES

We have decided to use black-and-white imaging to make our books more affordable. To ensure you have the greatest reading experience, we have included a QR code below the first image in our book, so you can scan the code to view the color version of the images in the entire book. If you scan the QR Code, you will be redirected to our website and immediately have a colored version of every image, graph, or table to view.

PART I

FREE BOOK!!!

Because this community has given me so much, I wanted to give back. So I'm giving away 500 free copies of my next book. To claim your free book please email ADMIN@ YOUNGINVESTORBOB.COM with the subject Free book!!!

CONTENTS

INTRODUCTION

"The most powerful force in the universe is compound interest."

Albert Einstein

Even if you feel you have little experience and money to invest right now, don't worry. You have the superpower that few older, financially secure adults have, and that is time. I added the Einstein quote at the beginning of this book as it is the most important thing you'll learn. Compound interest is your best friend. But only if it has enough time to work its magic. In simple terms, compound interest means money earned not just from your invested capital but also from the interest it produces. This means the money you invested now creates more and more money over time—like a snowball effect.

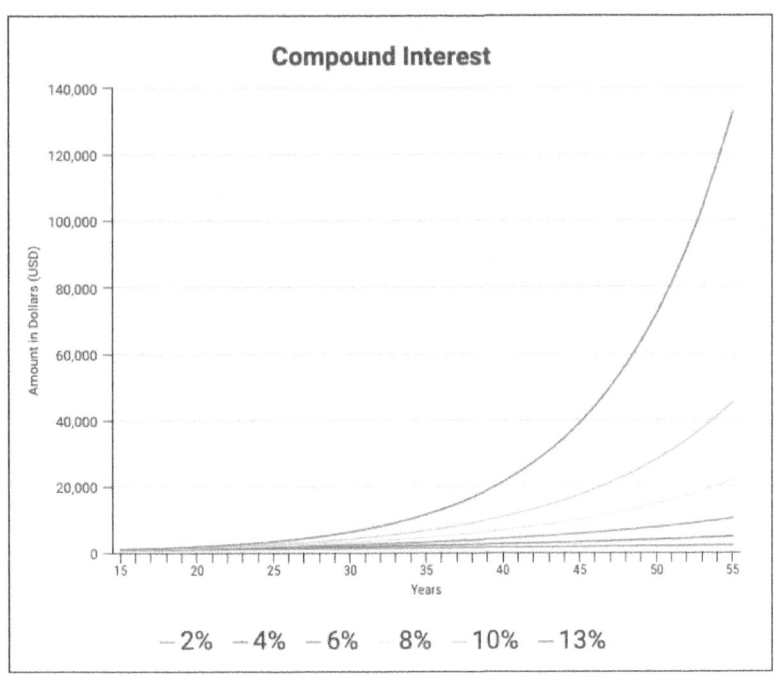

SCAN ME FOR COLOURED IMAGES

Take a look at the graph above. This highlights the power of compound interest excellently. This graph represents an initial investment of just $1,000.

Over time at different rates of return, the $1,000 will slowly increase more and more each year depending on the rate of increase. Generally, the stock market will produce a 8–10% yearly return. This is, however, not guaranteed. Some years are much worse, and some years are better. In the first 20 years, compound interest is not making much progress.

The major difference comes in the later years of the graph. Basically, this means to fully reap the rewards and benefits of compound interest, you need to be patient and consistently invest and hold money in the market. And this is where time comes in as a major factor. This is great news for you and me as we have plenty of time to let our money go to work. It is even better if you are 15 years old. It means you start getting **much** wealthier from your investments when you hit 35 years old. You can buy a house, travel, retire early—anything you want. And yes, 30– 35 years old is not super young, but much better than still being broke at 60. Also, it is worth mentioning that over 20–30 years, you will invest more than $1,000. So imagine the excellent results you can achieve with consistent investing.

However, one important thing to note is the amount of money in your investment account won't increase steadily forever. When things are going well in the stock market, you will experience growth of your assets. But, if the market were to take a downturn, the value of your total holdings would decrease. So this means that investing in the stock market does carry risk. You risk losing some or all of the money you have invested.

It's true (at least judging from the returns of the past 100 years) that if you wait long enough, the stock market will recover from any potential downturns. And the people who invested money back in 1900 have received an 8-10% average yearly return on their investments over 100 years. The important words here are "average yearly return," meaning the total annual rate of return divided by the number of years invested.

So, their money would have grown on average 8-10% each year, but this doesn't mean that every year yielded positive returns of 8-10%.

Some years could have been negative, like the 1929 crash that saw the Dow Jones (a famous stock market index made up of 30 US companies) decrease value by a whopping 89%. So, how does the market end up with positive returns? The years following this crash would have yielded greater positive returns than the total decrease in value the market experienced that year, resulting in net positive returns for the market index.

If this sounds overly complicated, fear not. All you need to understand here is the stock market can produce compound interest over time, but each year the market returns can be positive or negative, meaning it is possible to lose money from your investments. Thankfully in this book, you'll discover all the best techniques and strategies to ensure you have the best chance of earning positive returns from stock market investing.

Investing has allowed me to travel the world with the people who mean the most to me while I was still young enough to appreciate it fully. For other people, it would be raising a large family without ever worrying about money. Trust me; a life spent chasing money is no life at all.

The greatest investors like Warren Buffett manage a 13% average return. But even if you are an average investor at 8%, you are still destined for substantial financial success. There is no requirement to study finance at university or be a math guru or specialized financial expert. The people on Wall Street and the wealthiest 1% want you to believe investing is very complicated. So they always use a lot of jargon like bull vs. bear, gamma squeeze, portfolio rebalancing, obscure ticker acronyms, etc. They do this to make you believe it is too complicated to handle your investments yourself and instead let them manage your money.

The truth is, whether you are a shark on Wall Street or an average Joe like myself, we all have the same opportunity to build our investing knowledge. Sure the hedge fund managers have million-dollar salaries to work with. But this doesn't mean the little guy can't also be success-ful; you just have to believe in your ability. To show that anyone truly can find investing success no matter what background they are from, take a look at my own personal journey.

"Make money work for you." When I was younger, I had heard that sentence many times, and yeah, that certainly sounded great—for sure much better than working for your money like everybody around me was doing. But making it happen was a different story. Growing up as a young boy, I wasn't blessed with a good understanding of money, how to make money or what to do once I've made money. My parents worked extremely hard for everything we had, and my brothers and I were never left wanting.

But as I'm sure you can all agree, there is quite a difference between getting by and being wealthy. I noticed the difference between the rich and poor after the 2008 financial crisis hit. All around me, I saw people struggling to get by and working day and night just to survive. Even at that young age, I knew I wanted more in life. I wanted to be free from the stress of chasing money and constantly being broke. Some of us can spend our entire life chasing the next paycheck and never really have the opportunity to sit back and do the things that make us happy.

The desire to become free from this money burden compounded every time I couldn't buy the new game I wanted, and when I had to take the bus and couldn't afford the fun weekends away with friends. I hated seeing my family worry about money and stress about how we were going to afford to get by year by year. All these reasons fueled my mind, and I knew there definitely had to be another way to live.

I became obsessed with money and how to make it. I dreamed every day of being able to work for myself and have my own office where I would show up and leave when I wanted. I wanted to support my family, give them the best possible life, and travel the world as I pleased. To me, this is what life is about and not simply working until we are too old to have fun.

But at that moment, it was just a dream, and to make that dream a reality; I decided to take action. I picked up my first book on business and money and soon fell in love with the concept of investing. The idea that the money I earned from my job could be put somewhere other than the bank and could turn a profit for me while I did absolutely nothing was exhilarating.

I deliberately focused all my attention on being the best investor I could be. I had always been interested in movies about Wall Street and businessmen in fine suits, so I believed this could be the right path for me to find the financial success I desired.

During the early days, I read as many investing books as I could get my hands on. But I struggled in the beginning as there were so many different people with different ideas and opinions. What was the correct one, and who should I listen to? On top of the mountain of information available, there were also the scam artists and so-called gurus that I had to find out to avoid the hard way. As a young teenager, the concepts covered in the books were extremely hard to understand, and of course, it took me much longer than the average adult to piece together the teachings for myself.

Often, I felt like giving up as the challenge of investing seemed too great and difficult for a young person like me, but I decided to keep persevering. Fast forward 9 years, and I am much more financially secure than I once was. It didn't take me any fancy tricks and didn't happen overnight. But I have found the success I always dreamed of having. The key to my success was consistent hard work and learning to manage and invest my money wisely. Honestly, the only regret in my investing career is not having started sooner.

Today is very different from my teenage years. I am sure readers of this book know people around them getting rich speculating in crypto. Or maybe on Reddit meme stocks (wait, it sounded too old-fashioned, "investing in crypto"). Maybe it's a bubble or perhaps not, but people certainly hear a lot more about investing nowadays. Investing has become a hot topic in modern times, mainly because of more and more people having access to the internet and the vast amount of information available online. Thankfully, many people now realize that we don't need to slave away at a 9–5 job for 40 years to build our wealth. Just in case you were still a little unconvinced, let me assure you it is absolutely 100% possible for you to retire at the age of 40–50 if you invest correctly.

But it's not that simple, of course. For every investing success story, there is a horror story of hundreds of thousands of dollars evaporating overnight.

Or Robinhood blocking you from making a profitable trade just when it's convenient for hedge funds. So how can you be the lucky one? Well, this book aims to teach you the basics of how to get rich safely through stock market investing.

While occasionally referring to other investment strategies, I think the best way is still through investing in the stock market. You also might be wondering if this book will be relevant to teenagers and young adults and not just another complex investing book? The answer is yes! The Young Investors team and I are dedicated to informing the next generation of investors how to find their success and freedom through the stock market and other investing methods. Now that we have found our financial success, we want to give back to people similar to our younger selves. People who also dream of supporting their families and building a better future for themselves. I know the pain of not being able to find quality information that applies to teenagers.

Growing up, if I had found an investing book designed for my younger self, I would be much richer than I am now. So, to pass on this knowledge and ensure you are twice as successful as I am, the team promises to do everything in our power to provide the quality information you need to move along your investing journey. To improve your chances of success right away, we have divided our teachings on stock market investing into two books. The first part (Part 1) is what you are reading now. This book will focus on passive investing strategies and how the young investor can use them to get rich without any of the heavy lifting. With stock market investing, there are two main strategies: passive and active. In this part of the series on stock market investing, we will cover the passive strategy.

WHAT IS PASSIVE INVESTING?

The idea behind passive investing is to limit the amount of buying and selling of assets to increase returns over the long term. With every trade you complete, you will likely have to pay fees along with taxes. If you trade regularly, this will increase the amount of fees and taxes you must pay over time.

Passive traders want to limit the profits they lose, so they prefer a "buy and hold" approach to stock trading. They purchase assets in the stock market intending to hold them long-term, and they then hope the price of the assets over years and decades will increase. This means they will pocket a nice profit and not have to reduce these profits by overpaying on fees or taxes.

One very popular method of passive investing is to use indexing. As passive investors naturally feel it is difficult to "beat the market" (outperforming the benchmark's average annual return), they instead look to match the market performance. An index measures the performance of a subset of the stock market. A simple example I can give you is the S&P 500. This is a measure of the performance of the top 500 companies in the United States stock market, as chosen by the company Standard & Poor's. As the passive investor is simply trying to match the market, they would be happy to receive the average yearly return of those 500 companies according to the index.

So investors would find an index fund (don't worry, we break this fund down thoroughly in later chapters) that tracks the S&P 500, and this fund aims to provide the same return as those 500 companies in the index. What makes index funds passive is that they require little to no maintenance. No matter what happens in the market, the index fund will track the same companies in the index. This leads to lower trade fees, taxes, and management fees as the fund manager does not have to provide much maintenance.

These are all massive advantages of passive funds and also a major reason why passive investing often outperforms active investing over the medium to long term. It might be surprising, but it is very difficult to outperform the market. Even experienced investors and active fund managers struggle to beat the market because constantly choosing winning stocks yearly is very difficult. Even if you find a fantastic active manager, who picks the best stocks every year and averages a yearly return higher than the index, after the trade fees, taxes, and the manager has taken their cut, then your returns will likely be once again lower than the market average (Chen, J. (2021, May 19)).

Passive investing can be limited compared to active investing. And especially in bull markets (good market conditions), active investing can massively outperform passive investing. But over the long run, passive investing has the edge. And as most of you reading this book could potentially have 50 years of investing ahead of you, this strategy could be the one to make you wealthy beyond your wildest dreams.

Don't worry if active investing still sounds like something you want to try. We cover all bases in the second book (Part 2 of the series). Active investors will be more hands-on with their investments and regularly buy and sell **individual stocks** to try and achieve better-than-average results. We have left this information for Part 2 due to the difficulty involved with this strategy. Also, we believe the passive style is better suited to the young investor and will give you the best chance of success.

Remember, time is your superpower.

So without further ado, let's begin investing. However, before you learn how to make money by investing, you need to know just how powerful our minds can be regarding life and investing.

1

THE POWER OF MINDSET

*B*efore we get started with practical advice on investing, I need to clarify something important. Good investors are not smarter or more knowledgeable than bad investors.

Every time I lost money in an investment, it was not because I was not smart enough but because I failed to think clearly or control my emotions—usually both. Rich people think differently than poor people, not because they are rich. They are rich *because* their mind functions differently. I am, of course, not referring to people who got rich by inheriting a fortune from their family, as this isn't much of a skill. If you were in this situation, learning how to get wealthy would not be your concern.

So even before you start investing, you need to acquire the right mindset. But what does that even mean? A mindset is how you understand the world. People with two different mindsets can come to completely opposite conclusions about the same situation.

For example, let's look at a bad grade on a math exam:

At school, I would see it as proof that I was bad at math and should do something else. Another student will see it as the next thing they need to improve upon to get to the next level or grade.

I would say, "Yes, my classmates can do much better at math because they are amazing and so much better than me." Even though the grade was the same for both students, the reaction wasn't. I always assumed investing was simply a "numbers game," and I would not have the skills to invest correctly. The realization that anyone, including myself, could be good at investing took me many years to honestly believe. Only from reading many books and absorbing as much information on investing as possible did I finally start to understand that it is much more than just calculations.

FIXED VS. GROWTH MINDSET

Even if real life is more complicated than a simple math exam, we can simplify a little and divide mindsets into two camps: a fixed mindset or a growth mindset. **A fixed mindset** believes nothing can change. You either have musical talent, or you do not. You are privileged, or you are not. You are either born rich, or you will die poor. There is no room for change or improvement in this person's mind.

They believe some people will be lucky in life and succeed, and others not. Many people believe this, and I cannot blame them, as inequality and discrimination make us feel this way every day. Growing up poor, this is sure how it felt for me. Everybody I knew had a fixed mindset, stuck in unemployment or dead-end jobs, unhappy relationships, and so on.

If you compare this to a game, this person would be stuck on a low-level character for every mission. **A growth mindset** is the opposite. It is always looking for ways to get better, improving all the time. In a game, this is like leveling up quickly and using your XP points efficiently. Some people are even able to speed run it.

Growth mindset

The good news is that real-life works pretty much like a video game. The more you do something, the more skill levels you unlock.

A fixed mindset is like refusing to use your XP points and complaining the game is unfair. A growth mindset is using the XP to pick the best build possible.

The trick is to know you have XP points to spend and that you can max out how to obtain them. With the right mindset, you will make money, and more importantly, you can succeed even if you don't yet have a lot of money. Which I imagine is the case for most readers of this book and certainly was for me as a young boy. The unfortunate people stuck in a fixed mindset are cursed to spend life constantly feeling unfortunate and hard done by. People with a growth mindset truly have no limits to what they can achieve.

Changing your mindset is the ultimate cheat code in life. You level up faster, access more options, and get more done with less. The moment I unlocked that, everything started to change. Slowly at first (it does take time and hard work), but gradually I began to pick up momentum. Until today I am so fortunate that I can write books about the topic I love and share my knowledge with the young people who need it most. It all begins with believing that you can change not only as an investor but also wholly transform all aspects of your life.

What a growth mindset can accomplish

There is no greater example today of the growth mindset than Elon Musk. How can you not admire his sheer determination in life? Contrary to many other billionaires born into influential families, he had to go and earn everything he was given in life. Musk was born in South Africa. Growing up, he was bullied and beaten and often ended up in the hospital. He wasn't always flush with cash and grew up relatively poor. Now Musk could have given up and remained just as and where he was. He had all the excuses in the book, school troubles, bullying, and no money. But he didn't give up!

So Musk left South Africa, first for Canada, then America. He almost went into a Ph.D. specializing in the construction of electric batteries nearly a decade before starting with Tesla.

But he could not shake off the idea that *"there was this thing going on called the internet, and I had to be part of it."* His first taste of success came from building an internet start-up alongside his brother. During this time, he was sleeping in his office, eating a diet of instant noodles. To me, Elon is the incarnation of a growth mindset. Even from his humble beginnings, his success already felt like a logical goal to him, whereas many of us would never dream we could achieve it. The company he created and sold would later become PayPal and sold again to eBay for $1.5B.Now that he was a multimillionaire, he could have relaxed. Instead, he risked it again in two crazy ventures: Tesla, an electric car company, and SpaceX, a company that builds rockets.

At some point, both companies were only weeks away from going bankrupt. Taking risks and staying on the edge of running out of money had almost become a habit for him.

Out of the comfort zone

Do you know the saying "it's not rocket science?" Well, SpaceX was rocket science. Musk was an IT guy and a businessman. He knew nothing about physics or rocketry but wanted to get humankind to Mars. People with a fixed mindset said he should stay in what he was good at, software companies. Imagine the world where Elon Musk had just made some software instead of electric cars and spaceships.

Musk, the avatar of a growth mindset, knew nothing was impossible and made it happen through sheer stubbornness, optimism, and hard work.

Can mindsets be changed?

"Well, I am not Elon Musk, so I can't achieve what he has".

You know what, that's true. We will not all become the next Elon Musk, and that's fine. I cannot work 18 hours a day like him and still do a good job. What we can do is *think like Musk*. As it is very clear that Musk was not born this way, he made himself into the juggernaut he is today.

Like him, I also learned how to change my mindset and harness its power, and so can you" (Blystone, D. (2021, August 24)·

You need to adopt a growth mindset to become a successful investor to remove the shackles we put on ourselves. If we don't honestly believe that we can make and invest money, we will quit anytime we come up against any adversity or failure. You need to be willing to make poor decisions and learn from these mistakes. Every great investor you know would have lost money over their career and probably more than they would care to tell. Develop and use a growth mindset to navigate through those hard times, and you will undoubtedly become the success story you desire to be.

How to develop a growth mindset

Daily practice and patience are the most important steps to forming a growth mindset. You must constantly live your life with growth in your mind. It will be tricky at first, and some days you just won't feel so confident that you can improve on the task you are performing. Dust yourself off the next day and get right back after it. You purchased this book for a reason. You want to become a teenage investor; the reasons are your own. I can imagine you want to build a better life for yourself and your family, be free from working a boring 9–5 job and travel the world and experience everything it offers. The growth mindset is the first step on the road to reaching this freedom.

Below is a short list of how to practice a growth mindset daily and, of course, continue to research and practice the growth mindset as it can always be improved upon and is never perfected.

- Understand why you want to develop a growth mindset.
- Realize that we are limited; not everyone can play in the NBA.
- Begin to look at failure as an opportunity to learn and grow.
- Reflect at the end of the day; what have you learned from your actions?
- Don't look for the approval of others; this is for you!
- Be happy for the success of others.
- Take on more challenges; do something that scares you daily.
- Pay attention to how you speak to yourself and make it positive.

THE WEALTH MINDSET

The secret weapon of the wealthy

Let's talk about a wealth mindset and how to use it to our advantage. Besides looking at a wealthy person and seeing all the fantastic things they can do in life, have you ever sat back and thought, "yes, but how did they get there?" Well, if you were like me, I'm very interested in this question because it can inform us and guide our journey to riches. From reading many wealthy people's autobiographies, articles, movies, and watching YouTube videos to anything else, I could get my hands on. I noticed a pattern in many of their stories.

The interviewer will ask the wealthy man or woman, "So how did you reach this level of success?" As you can imagine, this is not an easy question to answer as these people have been in their careers for decades and even over half a century. So, of course, they can't pinpoint everything that made them who they are. However, one thing did jump out to me repeatedly, and this, of course, was their powerful mindsets. In particular, something I later found out was called a wealth mindset.

A wealth mindset is a lens through which a person can view the world. When viewing life this way, the person will begin to notice all the possible ways they could start to make money and all the ways they are currently wasting it. This individual has a set of beliefs, habits, and actions that constantly drive them toward the goal of growing their wealth. If this sounds easy, don't be mistaken. This involves an almost monklike sense of control. The fundamental difference between a successful and nonsuccessful person is the ability to fail, fail, fail and fail again but not stop working towards this goal.

A wealth mindset involves constantly looking for ways to improve your finances, spend less money, make more income, invest more of the money you have, remove wasted time, and constantly educate yourself on money/finances. If you were to break down the rich and successful investors we idolize and try to pinpoint some reasons for their success, these shared beliefs and actions would repeat time and time again. They are so simple, and we have all heard them thousands of times, but how many of us do them consistently?

1. **They set goals**. Patience is essential when setting goals. It might take a while, but they know where they are going and how to get there. Goals should be specific and actionable, like reading one book per month. Not "learn investing."
2. **They work as if they have $2 to their name.** To invest money, you first need to make money. For successful investors hustling never stops. Every successful investor had to learn to appreciate the value of hard work. If they had a paper route

early in the morning and could make it back in time for a second, they would do it. If they had time in the evening to help out in a local corner shop, they would use that time. They are no different from us, and we can do the same. If we hustle our butts off for a few years, it will be worth it.

3. They know the **difference between wants and needs**. A want is something that can be postponed. Beyond food and basic shelter, almost everything in life is a want. Warren Buffet is worth 100 billion dollars and still lives in a house he purchased in 1958 for $31,500. For most of us, saving a larger part of our income is the only reliable way to begin investing.

4. **They invest early in life**. If hard work alone were enough, there would be plenty of rich farmers, cooks, and coal miners. Wealthy people know how to make money work for them. Poor people unfortunately only know how to work for money.

5. **They keep learning.** A successful investor knows that times change all too quickly, and if they were to be left behind, they could easily begin to perform poorly. That's why research, education, and working on one's mindset can never stop. They always look to acquire new skills or perfect the ones they have.

Now, as simple as the points above are, if you were to begin working on each of them today and had the patience and the drive to work harder than everyone else, then who knows, you could be the next investing tycoon.

Poisons to the wealth mindset

Here are some of the biggest things to watch out for as they can deflate the strongest minds.

- **Thinking short term.** Getting rich is a long process. Shortcuts are the best way to *lose* money. This is why "greed is good" is a very bad motto. Greed makes you take shortcuts. That's the shortest way to lose money or go to jail. Jordan Belfort in *The Wolf of Wall Street* should not be your role model.
- **Fearing change.** Embrace new challenges. See problems as opportunities to shine over the competition. Don't give up on what did not work, and improve on what worked.

- **Not Looking for the path of least resistance.** I'm sure you have heard this saying many times before. But apply it religiously to your investing journey. Yes, work hard and make sure you don't take shortcuts. But at the same time, don't put any undue stress on yourselves. Sometimes it is better to take a step back and plan your journey rather than plowing ahead and making no real progress.
- **Time wasting.** We have 24 hours daily to be the best we can be. We sleep for one-third of our lives, and how much of the rest do we waste by not being productive? We might then lie in bed saying, "Man, I wish I could travel the world, but I don't have any money." DON'T waste your time; it is precious.
- **Getting into too much debt.** When it comes to the wealth mindset, you must understand that anything that is drawing money out of your account each month needs to be making you richer somehow. Don't use debt or loans to fund holidays or purchase new clothes. This is bad debt, and this debt and interest will work against you.

The wealth mindset builds the foundations for getting rich.

THE INVESTOR'S ROUTINE

"You'll never change your life until you change something you do daily. The secret of your success is found in your daily routine."

John C. Maxwell

A routine that will make you money

Scientific studies show that our routines will eventually lead to forming our habits, which are much more concrete and harder to change. Our habits will also impact our mood, and our mood will affect not just our day but also our productivity. So the value and importance of a daily routine if we wish to become skilled investors can't be overlooked (Loredo, A. (2022, January 3))·

Before we get into the importance of a set daily routine, one thing to mention is time off. Don't be fooled by the people who say, "I never take days off." Now I know there must be people who never stop working, but is this the life you want to live? It's definitely not the one for me. Every week I take at least one day, if not two, to do absolutely no work and you should try to do the same.

Growing up as a young boy interested in money and success, I often studied the people I admired. I wanted to figure out what exactly makes these special people different from you or me. Besides their wealth mindset and high intelligence, many businessmen attribute their success to a good daily routine and consistency. Look at the routine I created for myself when I was 18. I admit that I was very disorganized before making my first daily routine. My sleep schedule was messy, and I regularly slept under five hours a night. My productivity was low because my day was not planned out, and I wasted a lot of time during the day that I could have spent either making money or learning more about investing. Thankfully, this simple routine below helped me improve many of those problems.

- Wake up at 6 AM.
- Spend at least 2 hours a day educating myself on investing, money or finance.
- Go to school or work (8 hours).
- Exercise 30–60 minutes every day.
- Eat healthy meals.
- Sleep 8 hours a night.
- Meditate or pray once a day.
- Work on my side hustle for as long as possible each day.
- Make time for family and friends (maybe on weekends).

To help me stick to my daily routine and stay motivated, I also wrote down my long-term goals and why I started investing in the first place:

- I don't want to work a 9–5 job.
- I want to travel the world.
- I want to be a millionaire by 31.
- I want to give back to my parents and take care of my family.
- I want freedom in my life to choose what I do day to day.

The reason I chose those "rules" to live by was due to so many wealthy businessmen swearing by them.

Let's take a quick look at why those habits can increase your chances of success.

An Investing Scholar

Of course, this book will focus on passive investing; as the name suggests, it should be a "hands-off approach." But when we begin our investing journey, it pays to learn as much as possible about the topic. Even if we decide to invest our money passively (we would suggest that you do at the beginning of your career), we still need to be educated and make informed decisions.

Reading books such as this is a great start. Learn from our years of intense study and research to get a head start on your investing journey. When I began investing all those years ago, there wasn't much quality investing knowledge designed for a teenager like me. The books I read and the videos I watched were complicated to understand. Not only was it time-consuming to try and understand the information, but it was also intimidating. I often felt as though I was too young to learn how to invest.

But in reality, beginning your investing journey as a teen is possible. You have a lot of time to learn and develop your skills, plus you have lots of time to let your money work for you. So get started today by reading this book, but don't stop there. Also, invest in Part 2 of this book series when you are finished and keep on going. Even today, I constantly try to become a better investor by taking courses and reading books. Thankfully for you, we will break down what we have learned in a manner designed for a teenage investor. But don't shy away from those challenging and complex technical books, as even though you might not understand them immediately, they will help your investing over time.

Side Hustle

In simple terms, a side hustle is something you work on when you are not in school, and it is also different from a regular part-time job. The idea is to use your free time to make even more income that can be used, and in our case used to invest in the stock market. Take a look at your normal day-to-day life right now. How much free time do you currently have?

Do you like to play your PS5 or Xbox in the evenings? Do you spend a few hours on your phone each night? Can you find any time during your day that you could spend working on a side hustle?

My side hustle as a young teenager was giving some personal training classes to my friends who had just started resistance training. I have always been a big fan of playing sports and exercise, so why not put this passion to some use? As soon as I finished my standard job, I would use about 3 hours of my evening to coach some people and pick up a few extra dollars a week. It wasn't much, but trust me, it helped and allowed me to invest even more money in the stock market.

In today's modern world, we are blessed with the fantastic opportunities the internet has given us. Now people of all ages around the world are making thousands of dollars each month and, in some cases, earning enough money from their side hustles to replace their full-time jobs. If you are interested in starting a side business of your own and beginning to make hundreds of dollars per month immediately, we can help you. The Young Investor team has created a teenager's guide to making money online. In this short guide, we will give you 10 of the best methods of making money online today as chosen by our expert group of businessmen.

To invest successfully as a teen, we will first need to earn money to invest. So, we have deeded to give this document free to all our readers in the hope you too can begin earning thousands of dollars each month. If you want your free copy, please visit www.younginvestor-bob.com and start making money today. You can also scan the QR code on the back cover to be redirected to our site.

Thankfully there are so many options available for a side hustle: blogging, driving Uber, e-commerce, freelancing, coding, anything that boosts your income. That money should go directly into investments or savings. The guide provided above is an excellent start to your business career, but I won't discuss how you should go about creating a side hustle in this book. But look out for a future book for the young investor team on young entrepreneurship to take your business to the next level.

In the next chapter on money management, we will discuss further the importance of a job or side hustle. All of the tips above can be implemented into your routine. But it should be **YOUR** routine. Everyone will have different lives, so don't feel pressured into copying this template or any other famous investors' daily life. The example of my daily routine was used to show what worked for me and why those factors are important.

To help design your daily routine, The Young Investor team has created a daily routine template where you can easily plan your day and accomplish all the tasks on your to-do list. Go to www.youngin-vestorbob.com, download this free tool, and start implementing your daily routine today. Don't underestimate the power of your mind. This is the strongest tool you, as a young investor, have in your arsenal. If you work to develop a growth mindset along with a wealth mindset, form good habits and follow a daily routine. Over months and years, you will soon notice your life beginning to change for the better. You will no longer have a victim mentality, and if something goes wrong in your life, you will use it as fuel to push on.

Gradually you will begin to change your beliefs about yourself and money and form good habits around spending and saving. *Mindset* was chosen as the first chapter of this book because it is the most important aspect of the young investors' success.

The next chapter will tackle the second most important problem facing a teenage investor: how to make enough money to begin investing. Chapter 2 focuses on good money management and ways to increase the amount of money you have at the end of the month without having to work any extra hours. So, let's use our new and improved mindset and begin filling our bank accounts.

2

MILLIONAIRE'S MONEY MANAGEMENT

*W*hen it comes to getting rich, most people try to look up to billionaires like Elon Musk or Jeff Bezos. But I think this is often not helpful for practical advice. They made their money by being some of the world's best entrepreneurs and building trillion-dollar companies.

That might be you, but it's unlikely. So, what worked for them is not necessarily what the mere mortals like you and I can achieve. Instead, it is best to imitate millionaires. Most of them are self-made, and almost all reached that point with methods anyone can apply to themselves—no need to build the next Amazon or Tesla here. Instead, we will work on perfecting the right money management principles. One fundamental aspect almost all millionaires share is modesty. They do not live flashy lifestyles, and most people would never guess they are millionaires by looking at them. They shop at Costco, live in a comfortable but reasonably sized houses, and travel in normal planes, not private jets.

I always imagined millionaires to be like Leonardo DiCaprio in the *Wolf of Wall Street* movie. Flashy, brash, loud, wearing expensive suits and blingy watches and hanging out with models. Instead, the real millionaires look like your typical mom or dad in the suburbs. The flashy guys usually end up broke (they spend it all) or in jail (they did shady deals to keep up with their spending).

Often both. Unsurprisingly, the top models disappear quickly when the money is gone. So instead of trying to look rich by purchasing flashy clothes, new electronics, or new cars, focus on becoming wealthy by managing your money correctly.

SAVING RULES

You may have noticed the millionaire guy down the street or across the block in your neighborhood doesn't flash his cash too often. Sure, he might have a nice car and a big house, but have you seen him buy a new car every month? And if he does, trust me, he won't be your millionaire neighbor for long. Even the rich people of our society know that good money management and smart saving is key to success. So, let's look at some millionaire advice.

No matter how rich a man or woman gets (okay, if they are an oil billionaire, maybe not), you should always have an emergency fund fully prepared. Now you might wonder what an emergency fund is and why I need one? The books, articles, and interviews I have read about successful investors constantly stress the need to create an emergency fund or a nest egg. This is a separate savings account from your normal bank account, where you will deposit a set amount each time you get paid. The goal is usually to set aside 3–6 months of your wages in the event that you have a life emergency and need some extra cash.

Firstly, this is a great way to work on your money management and learn how to save a set amount each week or month. But why would extremely wealthy and successful investors still stress the importance of a nest egg? It will become more obvious once we discuss stock market investing in later chapters. But I will briefly overview the importance now. Suppose an investor were to skip creating an emergency fund and invest 80–90% of their income into the stock market. Now let's imagine the investor has a sudden life emergency. Perhaps they need to pay medical bills, or they need to repair their car, or any other unfortunate event you could imagine.

The investor has two options: take out a loan to cover the event's cost or pull the money they have invested out of the stock market. The first option will leave the investor paying back a loan with high interest for the coming months and years. This will leave them in a much worse financial state than they would have been before investing in the market. The second option is not much better financially if you don't leave your invested money in the market long enough and you are exposed to an unexpected downturn where the market could lose 10–20% of its value in a short time. This investor would then lose a good deal of invested capital as they can't wait for the market to recover and grow once again, as they need the money now.

The final reason will be discussed in more detail later in the book. But to avoid paying higher taxes and trade fees, you will want to leave the money in the market for a longer period of time. As teen investors, we might be lucky enough not to pay large medical bills or have high emergency costs. But trust me, nothing is worse than needing money ASAP and not having it. You also have to look at the positive side of creating a nest egg. Imagine you have constantly been investing money into the market, and then your friends decide to go on a holiday or to a concert. It would be a shame to miss out on such a one-off event just because we never put aside a little extra cash for an unexpected event.

A general saving principle is the 50/30/20 rule: 50% for necessities. 30% for wants, and 20% for savings. The average income for 16–19-year-olds in the USA is around $600 per month, so it breaks down like this:

50/30/20 RULE

TOTAL INCOME	50% NECESSITIES	30% WANTS	20% SAVINGS
$600	$300	$180	$120

I have never followed this rule as a young investor. I think it is good for people a little older who will have more bills to pay and a larger number of necessities. But for teenagers, necessities are likely lower. For example, if you have not yet left home for college or work, you are not paying large bills like rent, electricity, and heating. Perhaps your parents are kind enough to pay for the food you eat or cover other necessities we have as young individuals. So I like to suggest another rule. The 30/40/30 rule.

30/40/30 RULE

TOTAL INCOME	30% NECESSITIES	40% WANTS	30% SAVINGS
$600	$180	$240	$180

Note that I increased the "wants" as well. That's because life also needs to be enjoyed. The goal here is to get wealthy but also enjoy life along the way. If your savings strategy is too drastic, it usually will lead to poorer results as willpower will fade over time. Think of it as a strict diet; it is manageable for the first couple of days and weeks. But soon, you miss all those mouthwatering foods you have removed from your diet. And, eventually, you're more likely to give up on a diet and go back to old ways.

So moderation is key here to success. By all means, if you would like to save 90% of your income each month, then go for it. You will be on your way to becoming a successful investor in no time.

But if you are missing out on life to do this, I suggest a slight change to your approach. One crucial part of this step is once we begin to make more money—it could be from our investments or a better-paying job —people's natural instinct is to raise their standard of living. This means we will get a new car, apartment, or phone, and all of a sudden, we are saving less each month due to the increased spending. Millionaires know that to become successful, you must stick to the saving rules to ensure your investments and savings grow with your spending.

So let's follow the footsteps of the great investors or entrepreneurs that have already paved the way for us. Create your emergency fund and commit to filling the account before you even think of investing any of your income. The young investor should write down a goal of saving 3–6 months of their income (this will vary from person to person), and until they have a fully developed nest egg, they should not put any of their savings elsewhere. Trust me, the freedom you will have once you decide to begin investing will be worth it. From someone who has invested with and without an emergency fund, I can tell you firsthand that investing can be a worrying occupation without having some money to fall back on.

NEEDS VS. WANTS

I've mentioned above that spending increases over time along with our ability to make money. I mention this because it happens time and time again. People who win the lottery sometimes are broke again in a few years. NBA stars, some of the world's highest-paid athletes, go broke after retirement, and even megastars like Floyd Mayweather have had financial problems. If you are a young investor like me, you dream of one day retiring early rather than working into your 60s.

To make this happen, you need to love the idea of saving money and managing it correctly. To do that, we need to discuss our needs and wants and determine what goes into each category. I used to say, "I need a new phone." But my phone was not broken; it was just getting old. I did not *need* a new phone. I simply *wanted* a better phone. Similarly, I never needed a new game or console.

I could have carried on with life without it. I needed things like gas for my car, food, textbooks, medicine, insurance, work clothes, etc. Making the distinction is important because it allows you to put every dollar spent in the correct category for the 30/40/30 rule (or any rule you prefer). Needs are something you literally cannot function with-out. These include things you need to enable you to work like trans-portation or a good computer. Unfortunately, I had no clue how to organize my budget. I would get money and spend it on what I wanted, and when actual needs showed up, I was already broke. This meant zero savings.

Although I was working a lot, I made no progress money-wise. I can imagine a lot of you can relate to my younger self. I have been working since 15 and making a decent wage. I started out working for a local horse trainer. Being from the country, there weren't too many other options for a young guy. The work was hard and honest labor, with us only getting a day off once every 2 weeks. I busted my butt for a couple of years, and it wasn't all bad. I enjoyed the work, and I believe it was an important factor in helping me to create a strong work ethic.

My goal with getting the job was to save for college initially, and with a constant wage coming in for a couple of years, I was well on my way to achieving this goal. Unfortunately, as I reached my 18th birthday, I didn't have much saved in my bank account. To tell you the naked truth, I couldn't even remember what I spent most of my money on during that period. I didn't have any necessities as I lived in a small house with my parents, and I wasn't even driving a car yet. At that point in my life, I did not understood the importance of good money management and saving. If only I could go back now, I would have a much larger net worth today as I only began to learn money manage-ment and saving skills once I turned 18.

Thankfully, I can share my story with all of you readers, and hopefully, someone who was once in my shoes can learn something from my mistakes. Today, saving money can be simple. There are many tools out there that can monitor our spending and break down each category for us.

I prefer the old-fashioned way of monitoring my income and spending, as I feel it highlights areas that are positive and negative more clearly. The first step is to download your bank statements and analyze them. Each spending should be put into one of the next 2 categories: Needs and Wants. Take a look below for an example of possible needs and wants.

NEEDS VS WANTS		
	Need	Want
Textbooks	X	
Concert Tickets		X
TV		X
Work Computer	X	
Console/gaming computer		X
Internet access	X	
Fast Food/dining out		X
Meals for home cooking	X	
New clothes/shoes		X
Gas	X	

You will notice how some categories depend not on the items but on what you do with them and the quality of the purchase. A computer and internet access are both needs nowadays for study and work. The same with a cell phone and often a car if you do not have access to good public transportation.

But a top-of-the-line gaming computer or a fancy new car is a want. The cheaper version delivers what you need, and the nicer one delivers what you want. Here you will need to be very honest with yourself. Do you want to buy something because it will feel good to have? Is it something you want because others have it too? Or because "you deserve it?" Or do you need it and cannot live without the purchase? I am not telling you to live like a monk. Wanting nice things is natural and healthy. Being frugal does not imply being cheap. There is a part in the budget for the wants. We just don't allow those wants to ruin our future wealth.

When I started viewing my spending this way, it was liberating.

I was always frustrated with money, never managing to get everything I needed. When I began to understand money better, I soon noticed more and more money piling up in my account each month. Sure, I was spending less and less, but most of my savings were gained by cutting back on restaurant lunches and daily coffees from Starbucks. By Simply saying no from time to time when I had an urge to spend money on some silly item, I found true freedom and liberty from the stress of money.

Once again, The Young Investor team wants to do our best to help you as much as possible. Speaking for myself, I love monitoring my spending every couple of months. Firstly, I would download my bank statements across each of my accounts. Then I would use **The Young Investors Money Management Tool** to analyze my income and spending for that timeframe. This tool breaks down our wants and needs and shows you exactly where your money is going. I have been using this tool for years, which has saved me thousands of dollars. Grab your free copy at www.younginvestorbob.com and manage your money like a millionaire.

SPLITTING YOUR INCOME

Once you have analyzed your monthly spending, you will know how much money is needed to cover your monthly living expenses. For some, it will be 50% of income; for others, it will be as little as 20–30%. Depending on your situation, you should apply the 50/30/20 rule or another rule with a higher saving percentage. Some lucky teenagers have all their needs covered by their parents and can save up to 50% without sacrificing their "wants." So how do we put this rule into action?

Let's say you earn $600 per month (it could be more or less). Your employer may pay you weekly or monthly. As soon as you receive the money, divide it into 3 parts. Your first important step is to remove the amount from your income that you need for your living expenses, for example, $300 if it is 50%. Put that money aside in an envelope or a separate bank account. This is the "do not touch" part you will have available to pay your necessary monthly needs.

You are now left with $300 for everything else like your wants and savings. You might think that constantly monitoring your spending is a real pain in the ass. But once you build this good habit, it becomes another normal part of your life. Maybe once every month, you sit down for an hour and analyze your spending for the previous 30 days. Initially, every penny we save each month should be used to fill our emergency fund. Until we reach our goal of at least 3–6 months of income saved, we won't use this extra saved income for our investments. When the day comes, and the nest egg is full, we can put this saved income to use in the stock market. If the nest egg money has been used for an emergency for some reason or another, you should look to fill it back up once again before continuing your investment stream.

Trust me; something will always go wrong when you can afford it the least. Murphy's law is real. *If it can go wrong, it will.* So using the 50/30/20 rule, we have $180 each month to spend on whatever we like. You could split this money into four and have a small amount each week. Or you could use it all in one go or perhaps save a few months in a row to buy an expensive item you have your eye on, like a new console, holiday, new clothes, or anything else. I would recommend keeping the money in cash. This way, you visibly see the pile growing or shrinking in your wallet.

Debit cards make it easy for the money to fly away. Credit cards are even worse as they let you go negative and screw you over with the hidden interests (more on that later in the book). So feel free to start saving more and more each month in a slow and gradual process. Over time you won't miss those weekly lunches with friends much, and you can go without that daily Starbucks Americano. Eventually, being a little more frugal with your spending will become a habit, and you will notice the money start to pile up.

One of this book's promises is the ability to retire early. Even as a teen investor, creating good saving principles is one of the key methods to retiring early and finding financial freedom. If you are a heavy spender, you will have to constantly increase the amount of money you are capable of earning.

This might be easy for a successful CEO or an expert investor. But young investors like you and I might be unable to generate such large income streams. But we have a massive advantage if we can lower our expenses. Think about who will be able to retire first, the investing tycoon who earns $1,000,000 per year and spends $950,000 on flashy items or the sensible young investor who earns $100,000 per year after tax and only spends $25,000–$30,000?

HOW TO RETIRE EARLY AND FIND FINANCIAL FREEDOM

I have a goal that I have not yet shared with you. This is to have the option to retire before I am 40 years of age. This would mean I have enough money saved or passive income streams (such as investments) that pay me enough to support my family and I. Sure; this might sound a little early for retirement. But trust me, this is 100% possible, and if you wanted to go crazy, you could probably retire before you are 35.

In Book 1 of the series, we will show you how to accomplish one aspect of finding financial freedom: generating passive income through our investments. Of course, Part 2 of the book will also show us how to make our money work for us by actively picking our investments. And to be clear, you don't have to be either a passive investor or an active investor—you can be both. I enjoy actively researching and picking my own stocks to invest in. But I still hold most of my investments in passive investment funds (more to come on passive investing in Chapter 5).

So we know we want to begin making more money and possibly living off the investment capital for the rest of our lives. But that alone will not allow us to retire early. Another part of early retirement is an excellent saving strategy. Especially as young investors, we will need to become excellent at saving our money to enter the stock market. But these saving principles must continue, even when we start making some real profit from our investment. It can be tempting to spend, spend, spend as soon as we see our bank accounts growing. But if you are like me and wish to retire early, we need to control our spending throughout our lives.

Of course, this doesn't mean having no fun, but we also can't buy a new Rolex every week. You will need a plan to achieve your early exit from the workforce. Think about how much you would like to spend each year after retirement. For example, I want to spend $50,000 per year. The average life expectancy for men in the United States is about 76 years old (O'Neill, A. (2022, February 2)). That means to retire at 40; I would need to have saved $1,800,000. Of course, that assumes I earn no other money between the ages of 40 and 76. But of course, with my investments and side business, I will also be earning passive income that can substitute for all those savings (Lake, R. (2022, March 28)).

So you see, it is possible to retire early. There are many ways to do it, and you could decide to go all out with the saving approach. It will be difficult and leave you somewhat vulnerable once you retire, but it is possible. Or you could become an expert investor over the years and continue this into your retirement. And sure, this approach might seem like work. But trust me, once the hard years of learning the art of investing are over, it becomes second nature and a lot of fun.

The final option I mentioned above for our early retirement strategy was a side business. This will be covered in much more detail in our upcoming book focused on teen entrepreneurship. So stay tuned!

PRACTICAL TIPS

I focused this chapter on budgeting and wants vs. needs because if you do not understand this chapter, no matter how much money you make, you will always be broke. Still, the younger you are, the smaller your income is. You likely only have a part-time job, no qualification or experience, no network, no diploma, and everything combines to limit the money available. The only good part is that lower expenses generally come with younger age.

So it is essential to use any trick to save more and spend smarter. It is also an excellent habit to develop and keep for the future.

Remember, those turning into millionaires generally have a surprisingly modest lifestyle. A vital part of building wealth is avoiding serious debt—especially credit card debt. Interest rates on credit cards are so high that they will prevent you from ever getting rich. There is almost no way to invest and get returns high enough to counteract the interest you need to pay on the credit card.

The math is very clear in this case. Let's imagine you have a high credit card debt and are paying back 20% interest of your initial loan each year. Let's imagine you invested the same amount of money as the loan you received in the market. Somehow you are pulling a 20% return from the stock market (almost impossible for even the experienced investors), then you will just about cover your interest payments for the year.

Another big money sink is all the subscriptions we pay. Corporations have gotten smarter. We used to buy software and movies on a once-off basis. Now they offer us a very large catalog for a "small" fee per month, and we happily pay the "lower" price. Except if you pay for cable, Netflix, Disney, Spotify, etc., you can easily end up with $100 per month or more. That's $1,200 in a year. You could save that or put it toward other wants you will enjoy more and keep for the long run, like the down payment on a second-hand car or buying a brand-new P.C.

A third big-money destroyer is food. One way to lose money is to spend it in restaurants, bars, and fast-food joints. I get it; this is fun, easy, and doesn't feel that expensive. But think about it. These taco and burger chains can open tens of thousands of restaurants, employ millions of people, and pay fat dividends to their shareholders. And that's with **your** money.

On top of that, we all know it is not healthy. So you risk reducing your energy on top of spending too much. Another thing is to limit junk food and buy good ingredients like fruit, vegetables, and meat (or a substitute if you're vegan). Cooking meals yourself from scratch and packing lunch go a long way to saving more money.

This chapter is full of tips, tricks, and tools—designed to increase the amount of money we have in our savings and bank accounts each month. If you master good money management principles at a young age, I can guarantee you will never be broke again. Living within your means is a superpower for the young investor. Rather than wasting $250 a month on things that bring us momentary joys, such as food, clothes, games, or nights out with friends, if you were to invest this money instead, you would be well on your way to becoming wealthy.

As teen investors, our biggest challenge is creating capital for us to invest. We will need a part-time job or some method of creating income for ourselves like a side business. Even if you are too young to begin working, help out around the house or neighborhood, or pick up any extra chores you can. If we sacrifice in our early teens and 20s, we will not have to work so hard or at all in our later years. So once we have mastered our money management and are on our way to filling our nest egg, it is time to talk about investing, we will start with a very important step and that is learning to design our investment strategy.

3

INVESTMENT STRATEGY

*S*o far, this book has taken us through how to construct a mindset designed for success. We have also learned the power of good money management principles; this will provide us with the valuable funds needed to begin investing. But once you have the money saved, where do you begin?

A great place for any investor to begin their journey is to construct an investment strategy. In simple terms, this means a consistent approach that a person can take to reach a desired level of success while taking a level of risk that will allow them to sleep at night. You need an investment strategy to guide you on the decisions you make as an investor. Sure, you could skip the investing strategy and blindly begin to purchase assets on the stock market. But do you think this will lead you to success?

A well-thought-out investment strategy can help someone reach their goals much faster, safer, and in a more realistic manner. So what does an investment strategy involve? It can mean lots of things. What do you want to invest in? What goals do you want to achieve? How soon would you like to achieve these goals? Would you like some help with your investments? What is your risk tolerance? And so on. Don't worry if all of this seems very confusing. I will break down each aspect and assist in creating a perfect investment strategy tailored for you and your needs.

Where should I begin?

You have taken your first step to become a young investor; you have purchased this book and are willing to learn. So let me ask you, why did you purchase this book? Sure, you wanted to learn how to invest in the stock market. But why do you want to learn how to invest in the market? The answer to this question will differ for every individual, so don't worry if your reasons don't match your friends or the people you see online. Everybody will have different motivations for building wealth. I began investing because I feared working a 9–5 job for the rest of my life. I wanted more freedom; I wanted to travel and see the world while I was still young and full of energy. Another key reason was to take care of my family.

I'm sure many of you can relate to the goals I have discussed here. This is the "why" of my investing journey. It is more important than you might think. On those days you feel tired, stressed, worried, and want to quit, these goals are the driving force that will keep you on the path to investing success. Knowing the reasons why you invest will determine how you invest.

For example, if your goal is to save enough money to help buy a car, then you need a strategy that delivers results in a maximum of a few years. Since the purchase is only a few years away, you will likely be willing to take less risk, as you will have less time to recover from any down markets. Whereas if your goal is to purchase a house in 10 years, a more long-term approach is better where you might like to take on more risk in the hopes of higher returns.

Suppose the goal is to ensure a safe retirement in 30+ years, lots of up and down along the way matter very little. But high yield compounding over time will bring fantastic results. As with many things in life, your investment strategy will change over the years. If you think about it, a person in your shoes who might still be in high school will have much less responsibility. So you might want to take more risks with your investment strategy.

But in 20 years, you might be married with kids and have way more responsibilities, which will change your strategy. So remember the power of why we began this journey. If you want those reasons bad enough, you can't fail.

TRADING OR INVESTING? SPECULATING OR INVESTING?

There is some confusion about what investing means. You might hear people saying they invest money in their homes. Or that they started investing by day trading. There is plenty of jargon and conflicting definitions. While different people might not share my opinion, I think it is important you know the difference. When someone is *investing*, they are betting that a *productive asset* will bring them extra money. This asset can be a rental flat or a share of a profitable company. What brings returns on investment is that the asset is productive. If the company that you hold increases the sales of its products, its share price will increase. This is known as a capital gain.

If you own property and all across town rent is rising, you could also stand to make a profit due to the asset increasing in value. An asset simply means a possession of an individual or company. This asset may rise or fall in value over time, but you hope it eventually turns a profit —and don't worry—we will soon discuss all the many different passive assets the stock market has. Because the assets are productive, investing is safer than speculating. An apartment is worth something because having a place to live is valuable. A company is worth something because its employees produce something of value to the world. When someone *speculates*, they are betting someone else will buy the asset at a higher price.

Collectible cards have no value in themselves. It's just ink and paper. The only way to "make money" is to find someone ready to buy it at a higher price. Frankly, most cryptos are the same. This is not saying that speculating is inherently bad or dangerous. But it is riskier because there is no underlying production of something valuable.

If no one buys the collectible card any longer, its value is zero. Real estate or shares of good companies generally won't go to zero because they can make money anyway—even if no one wants to buy them from you.

When buying stock, you can speculate, invest, or maybe a bit of both. So depending on your investing style, you will either be an investor or a speculator (trader in modern terms). An investor buys a stock because they think the ownership of a percentage of that company is worth something. After all, the company is or hopefully will be profitable.

The future cash generated by the company and given to its owners (the people owning the stock) is the reason for the investment. A trader buys because they expect someone else to buy back the stock at a higher price. The trader may not like the company itself, but this is irrelevant to their strategy.

Another difference is that traders tend to have a much shorter hold period (how long they hold the asset). Day traders bet on change over just one day. Others might trade over the month or the quarter, but the goal is a quick result in days or weeks. Most investors will own a stock for one or several years, or maybe even decades. I am an investor, and that is how I get money to work for me. Some people prefer trading, but you need to know that data from trading platforms shows that more than 80% of traders end up losing money over the course of a year (Lyck, M. (2020, December 28)).

With these odds, no wonder so many people refer to trading as gambling. This is because trading does not rely on the underlying company's profits; this is a zero-sum game. By that, I mean your gains are someone else's loss.

Sure, people get rich trading, but the few who achieve it are thanks to the many losses of the majority. It is very hard, and I prefer to play a game where most players win rather than trying to get lucky. My investing routes come from a traditional approach, and in this book, I won't be discussing how to trade in the stock market. There would be too many contradictions for both myself and you as the reader to have an enjoyable learning experience.

RISK

I will define risk as to the permanent loss of money. It can happen two ways:

1. The stock goes down and never recovers.
2. The stock goes down, and you sell before it recovers.

Both will happen to you at some point. The hope is to have it happen as rarely as possible. What you need to know is how high your risk tolerance is. This simply means how much risk you are willing to take personally and financially to reach your investing goals. To determine that, I think you must first go back to your goals.

Let's imagine your goals are essential to your life, and you can't afford to lose the money you invest. You will likely have a low-risk tolerance because of this, and to help you sleep at night, you will choose low-risk investments. As you can imagine, a low-risk investment strategy is a trade-off. Usually, a person who chooses to invest in low-risk assets understands that they will get lower returns on their investment. Low returns simply mean less profit from your investments. This makes sense—why else would an investor decide to take more risk? It is in the hopes of higher rewards.

You must also understand your personality. Do you love risky sports, roller coasters, and anything adrenaline-filled? Then you probably can stomach more risk. If you have a quiet personality or have trouble dealing with anxiety, stressing out about your investments will not be something you can easily withstand. Ask yourself what your relationship with money is? Are you always worried you won't have enough money to support your needs and wants? Or are you a carefree spender who doesn't focus on how much is in their account? If you fear losing money and your investments begin to sour, you will most likely panic and sell off your assets.

Now, as we have seen, this is one of the ways we can lose money from our investments. To sell when the asset's price is down, you lose money. In this case, you might have purchased the asset for $100 and, in a panic, sold it for $75. This means you would lose over $25 once taxes and trade fees are taken out. Of course, the time will always come to sell some of our investments. But if we constantly buy into the stock market and we sell every time it takes a downturn, then we are almost guaranteed not to make a profit.

So if you think you might be likely to panic sell, you may be better off with some lower-risk investments. But don't worry; this book will help you identify what investments are right for you. The higher your risk tolerance, the more you can invest in a stock that might go to zero (the company goes bankrupt) and with high volatility.

Volatility is how dramatic the ups and downs of the stock price are. I'm sure you have seen a company's stock price graph. They are constantly going up and down as people purchase and sell shares of the companies. Generally, a more volatile company would be earlier in its life. For example, a new start-up company that has just recently begun trading on the stock market will have much more volatility than the stock price of Coca-Cola.

This is due to Coca-Cola's long history of good performance. They have solid historical sales and a good brand that has sustained them for years. This means they are more likely than not to continue doing good business. A person with a high-risk tolerance will be capable of holding firm, even if their investments are down 50% in a week. This ability can lead to higher returns from their investments, as the more volatile companies can usually create some great returns.

However, this high tolerance to risk can also lead to greater losses. Because if you constantly take higher risks, you will eventually find a loser and take a loss on your investment. Unfortunately, there is no set approach to investing, and people worldwide will differ in their philosophies. This is normal and nothing to worry about. We can only control our decisions, and the best strategy for us is the best one for us.

Types of risk

The biggest risk an individual investor exposes themselves to is business risk. When they buy stock, they need the company to keep operating and continue making money. If the company loses too much money, it will go bankrupt, and the stock will be worthless. A company with a lot of debt is also more at risk of bankruptcy. Debt can be described as the amount of money a company or individual might owe to another person or bank. For example, if the company decided to take out a loan to purchase and construct a new office building, they would then owe the loan issuer the money they borrowed plus interest payments.

So it can be exciting to bet on a promising start-up and hope to multiply your money by times 10 or 100. But as so many start-ups fail in a few years, it is very hard to pick the right one. Suppose you put your money into more stable businesses with a long history of making a profit. In that case, you will be less likely to make millions from that investment, but you are more likely to make some profits, and it's seen as a safer option (Chakrabarti, R. (2017, June 14)).

I learned all this the hard way over years of investing in single start-up companies with the hope of striking gold. I was taking on a massive amount of risk and hoping for a large reward at the end. Risk and investing go hand in hand; you can't invest without some level of risk. Often you will hear people ask what your risk tolerance is? This means how much risk you are willing to take with your investments. So now that you understand risk and investing let me turn the focus over to you. Ask yourself whether you will be more comfortable investing in low, medium, or high-risk investments. Don't worry if you can't answer that question immediately; developing your risk tolerance can take time.

TIMEFRAME

I just mentioned volatility, and this is important regarding your time horizon. If you invest money that you will need in 20 years, volatility is irrelevant.

Who cares if you had one very bad year 12 years ago? As long as your *average* compounding rate is 7–10% (average returns for the stock market for the last century), you will get a lot richer (Luthi, B. (2021, November 4)).

The average compounding rate can be broken down simply into how much your investment grew in one year or over a longer time. If you initially invested $1,000 in an ETF (exchange-traded fund, don't worry, we will explain this in Chapter 5) and one year later, the fund's price is now worth $1,100, then the investment's value would have risen 10%. Skip ahead 5 years, and the price has gone up $100 each year. Then you would have an average compounding rate of 10%. But what if you were unwilling to hold your investment for a long time? Say you are saving for college and can't afford to ride out the bad times in the market; a temporary down price will turn into permanent losses.

Actually, below a 1-year time frame, this is closer to trading than investing. Many would advise against selling investments in such a short period of time—aside from not having enough time for a down market to recover, you will also pay a higher amount of capital gains tax. Of course, we at The Young Investor are not tax advisors, so the level of information we can provide here is minimal. Anything we do provide throughout this book is simply for educational purposes. You should talk to a qualified professional if you need help with tax or any other part of your finances.

With that said, it is commonly known that if you hold an investment for longer than one year, you are subjected to long-term capital gains tax. Whereas anything you hold shorter than a year, you pay short-term capital gains (Internal Revenue Service. (2022, February 3)). Your income level will also play a factor in determining how much tax you pay. But the important thing to realize is the longer-term capital gains tax is at a lower rate, so less of your investment income will go to Uncle Sam.

So, what does a short-term investment timeline mean for our investment strategy? If you only have a few years until you hit the goal you are saving for (a car, for example), then the investments you make need to help you save rather than create massive profits.

This means those investments would need to be less risky. This safety is important because you will lack time to allow market volatility to recover if things go bad. This is another aspect you must consider when designing your investment strategy.

So ask yourself, when will I need the money I am investing? And am I investing for a particular goal? Make sure to give your goals a timeline.

For example, if you are saving for college, it will look a lot different than saving for retirement. So try to figure out if you would like to be a long-term or short-term investor—maybe even a little of both?

PASSIVE INVESTING

In 2019 passive investing made up half of all publicly traded assets on the U.S. stock market. Passive investing aims to match a broad market index or set of indices. An index can be considered an imaginary portfolio containing a certain type of asset that matches a segment of the financial market. For example, one of the best-known indexes on the market today is the S&P 500. This index tracks the performance of the 500 latest companies in the United States.

So, the fund manager would purchase shares of the 500 companies, and then people who buy into the fund can own a fraction of those shares (Chen, J. (2021, May 19)). In a later chapter, we will discuss more index funds like the ones that track the S&P 500. But for now, let's take a closer look at passive investing. Since these passive investing funds were created, what has made them so popular with investors?

Of course, the added diversification an investor gets from the funds is welcome. The ease at which an investment can be made and maintained is a real plus for time savers. The incredibly low fees, compared to the ones that active managers charge can increase profits dramatically. Let's assume an active fund manager charges a 1% annual management fee and a passively managed fund only charges a 0.1% fee. Even if the actively managed fund outperforms the passive fund, the large fees can reduce the gap or even put the passive returns ahead.

But perhaps the greatest reason of all becomes apparent when you look at the overall performance of active vs. passive in the last decade. The S&P 500 has reported that fewer than 15% of actively managed funds have outperformed the market (Bloomberg. (n.d.)). In the short term, say a year or perhaps two, active managers tend to do well and beat the market. But as time goes on, it becomes more and more difficult for them to maintain this excellent performance. According to the S&P 500 global, the trends worldwide are much similar in favor of passive. (The active vs. passive debate 2020, January 13)).

ACTIVE INVESTING?

It's important to realize that many of the fees involved with active investing come from using active mutual funds. Expert analysts and a fund manager maintain these funds. Of course, these people will need to be paid for their services, which can reduce the amount of money you make from your investments. But what if you were to invest in companies actively by yourself? In truth, it is still extremely difficult to beat the market, as choosing winning stocks over the long run is a very difficult thing to do. But if you manage to strike gold, you could receive massive returns from one or two smart investments.

I suggest a small fraction of your portfolio be dedicated to active investing. If you like the idea of picking your stocks and enjoy the research involved with the process, then maybe allowing 10-20% of your portfolio to be actively managed by you or a fund manager could be a good option to add a little flair to your investing. A good way to determine if choosing your own stocks or bonds is right for you is to ask yourself if you truly love learning about investing. Research into how to invest and what investments are best is crucial to becoming a successful active investor.

This method involves reading companies' balance sheets, annual reports, current affairs, market trends, news sites, and any other information that might tell the investor if the company's stock is a buy or sell. This investment might seem very appealing to you, but it is important to realize that this method is extremely difficult.

Even the best and brightest brains on Wall Street often struggle to "beat the market" (this means outperforming the average stock market performance). So, if experienced investors struggle to choose winning stocks, then perhaps this isn't the best method to begin your journey with.

Active investing works best if you find a sector or industry in which you already have a lot of interest or passion. This makes the research of the industry and companies much more enjoyable, and you will already have a head start on the competition. But don't focus so much on the active investing style at the moment. After all, this part of The Young Investors Stock Market Investing series is about passive investing, so we will explain how you can use this method to increase your wealth.

We believe that this strategy is much more suited to the teen investor. It increases diversification and reduces the risk an investor takes. Don't worry too much about those terms, as we will explain much more in Chapter 5.

ADVISORS

But apart from actively choosing your own stocks to invest in, many different options are available to the modern investor. Historically professional financial advisors have undertaken the task of managing people's money. These professionals will take the money you give them and invest it for you. This removes the need to research, investigate and maintain the investments you make.

Some people love having an expert invest their money for them. They feel that with their level of experience, their money would be better off in somebody else's hands. However, before you grab your laptop and find yourself a financial advisor, there are some important things a young investor should know. If you are starting on your investment journey, then the amount of money you have is probably quite low. This becomes an issue when trying to hire a financial advisor, as many won't accept your business unless you have a certain amount of money to invest.

For some of the larger financial advisors, unless you have $250,000 to invest, they won't accept your business. Even for the advisors that don't have account minimums, the fees for the majority can be way above the average young investor's price range. Other methods of charging their clients fees include a set 1% fee on assets managed. So whatever you hold in the account, the manager will charge 1% of those assets yearly. Other ways include a set yearly rate, usually between $2,000–$7,000 on average or $200–$400 hourly. So as you can imagine, this method might be out of a teen investor's price range.

However, there is no need to panic; financial advisors are unnecessary to become a successful investor. Many believe that by using a more passive method with our investing, we stand to make more money than most professionals on Wall Street. Burton Malkiel wrote in his 1973 book *A Random Walk Down Wall Street* that "a blindfolded monkey throwing darts at the stock listings could outperform the pros" (Malkiel, B. G. (2003))·

Robo advisors

Many trading apps are now offering the service of a Robo-advisor. This is A.I. (artificial intelligence) that will ask you multiple questions to understand your wealth, risk profile, time horizon, and goals. Then the software will come up with personalized suggestions depending on your responses.

Robo-advisors offer advice to millions of people at once and have an entire team of professional investors and programmers building them. So they are surprisingly good at offering personalized recommendations. These Robo-advisors can be a great option for the young investor as they remove the massive fees that a human, financial advisor may charge. However, It is important to realize that the level of advice you get from the robot-advisor will be much less specific.

The algorithm will give many people the same advice and lead to many people making the same investment decisions. But it is important to remember the greatest investors like Warren Buffet have made their fortune by going against the crowd.

I will discuss this option further in the final chapter of this book, as these Robo-advisors can be a great option to help you begin your investing journey.

Investment strategy round-up

The likelihood of success with investing is increased if you take the time to create a detailed investment strategy for yourself. Take a look at your current situation and where you want your investing career to take you. No two people will have the same investment philosophy, so don't worry if your friend has some different ideas on how to be successful.

Begin by asking yourself what your goals are? These goals will be important to guide you along your journey. It is important to know what we are trying to achieve, as it will impact what investments we decide to make. Then, how much risk are you willing to take to get you to those financial goals? The ideal level of risk for you is something that gets you what you desire while not worrying about losing your money.

As with everything in life, time is a crucial factor. When will you need this investment money? Will you be making more short-term or long-term investments? Then, the age-old battle of active or passive investing will have to be decided on. Ask yourself what approach sounds best to you, and ensure you understand the concepts fully before deciding.

Remember, it doesn't have to be one or the other, you can invest using both strategies. Now that we have covered how to design our investment strategy, let's use this information to create our investment portfolio in the next chapter.

4

A WORD FROM THE AUTHOR

*D*ear Reader,

    I hope you are enjoying my book and learning about the stock market and how you can use it to make money.

If you are enjoying our book, please leave a review of our book on Amazon.

This is free, only takes 60 seconds, and will truly make my day. I look forward to reading your review. If you can't review our book, why not ask your parents or guardian - whoever purchased the book to leave a review?

Please scan the QR code below to be redirected to our review site on Amazon.

Thank you so much!

5

BUILDING YOUR PORTFOLIO

$\mathcal{Y}$ ou might have heard of the term "portfolio." This sounds fancy, the kind of thing people in expensive suits talk about around expensive drinks in a New York office. The reality is that anybody that saves and invests money has a portfolio.

A portfolio contains all the assets you own. Defining what an asset is can be a little confusing. Simply put, an asset is something that you or a company owns that is valuable. So a car is an asset, and owning a flat or a house is also an asset. So it helps to think of your investment portfolio as an imaginary warehouse where you can store all your assets under one roof.

I always like to use that analogy because it describes something that sounds complicated, like an investment portfolio, in very simple terms. Let's say you want to hold 80% of your money in stocks and the rest of your capital in cash. This would mean your portfolio contains 80% stock with a fraction of your portfolio in cash, for example, 20%.

This chapter will explain precisely how you can design an investment portfolio. But why is it so important to create and maintain a good portfolio? Your investment portfolio will contain all the assets you choose to invest in and hope they make you money.

If you were to ignore your strategy and dive right in, you might end up with a bunch of funds that track young start-up companies. This would mean that you unknowingly just created a very high-risk portfolio. The best portfolio brings you to your financial goals ASAP while taking the least amount of financial risk. But apart from risk, a good portfolio should also offer diversification (O'Connell, B. (2021, December 8))·

Now we will cover what diversification is in more detail. But the idea is to hold different types of assets across multiple industries and sectors to protect you from a downturn in one of those assets or sectors. For example, if you were to hold an ETF that tracked the fashion industry in the good times, this would be a great option as they tend to outperform other industries in bull markets. But if a recession were to roll around, this industry would be hit hard and worse than many others. So to diversify and reduce the loss you might take, you could invest in something that is "evergreen," like healthcare. Whether times are good or times are tough, people will always need medicine and treatment (Jackson, A.-L. (2021, July 30))·

Finally, a well-thought-out portfolio can offer you good asset allocation—meaning the amount of your money you would like to invest into stocks, bonds, or hold in cash. This is a crucial factor that will tie into your investment strategy. Then to keep this asset allocation uniform, we will also have to "rebalance" it from time to time.

Let's look at a rebalancing example. Say we wanted to hold 75% of our assets in stocks and 25% in bonds, and stocks go on to perform well that year. Now suddenly, our stocks make up 85% of our portfolio and bonds only 15%. To get back to our original 75:25 split, we need to rebalance the portfolio. To allow the portfolio to find its original balance, we would need to sell some of our stocks and purchase more bonds until we have the 75:25 split again.

ASSET TYPE AND RISK

Every type of asset carries a different level of risk. Some are very safe, and some are insanely risky, with plenty of middle ground. This makes intuitive sense. Investing in a small start-up with an idea is riskier than buying shares of Apple. Lending money to the U.S. government is safer than lending money to an almost bankrupt company. From the lowest risk to the highest, assets can be categorized in something like the list below. In this section, I have decided to leave out things like real estate investments but keep an eye out for our upcoming book on the topic because real estate investing is another fantastic way of making yourself wealthy.

SAFEST/LOW RETURNS/LOW VOLATILITY

–

Cash/Bank account
Public bond funds
High-yield bond funds
Equity funds
Gold/precious metals funds
Growing dividend stock funds
Foreign bond funds
Large corporation stock funds

–

RISKIEST/HIGH RETURNS/HIGH VOLATILITY

–

Medium-sized company funds
Small-sized company funds
Foreign stock funds
Leveraged stock investing
Options/Futures/Shorting stocks

-

One of the safest investment categories is **bonds**. Bonds are basically a **loan** made by you to the receiver of the loan. When buying a bond, you act as the bank: you take your cash and give it to someone else.

The receiver of the money can be a government, a city, or a big corporation. In exchange for giving them the cash, they promise to give your money back plus interest.

A bond is a rock-solid contract. They **have to** pay you back. The amount of interest is fixed in the contract and cannot be changed. The duration of the bonds is also fixed, so they pay you X% of the total every year until they pay back the sum at a fixed date. So the only risk for the bond owner is if the issuer goes completely bust. Bonds are considered safe because cities and governments rarely tend to do that. The safer the borrower of the loan, the lower the interest percentage the bond will give you. The very high yield bonds are quite similar to stocks and are usually created by companies with money trouble and a high risk of bankruptcy.

So, for example, if you were to purchase a bond from the United States Treasury (Treasury bonds), this is much safer than a bond purchased from a goldmine in South Asia. You may notice from the list above the word *funds* appears quite often. A bond fund is simply a brokerage firm or entity offering a collection or group of individual bonds for you to invest in. A key distinction between active and passive investing would be how the fund was constructed. For example, if the fund was designed and is maintained by a "fund manager," and the fund employs analysts to research the investments that the fund makes—this is then known as active investing.

Often this active management of a pool of people's money is known as a mutual fund. We will cover this in much more detail in Book 2 of this series. But what is the passive version of this bond fund? The passive nature used to design the fund would be the difference; the brokerage firm offering the bond fund would track an "index" of bonds rather than actively choosing their own. We will dive deeper into Chapter 5 on index funds and this method of investing. But the key thing to understand here is that the fund manager is required to do no research or maintenance as they are simply tracking the bond index.

This fund is hence passively managed and falls into a passive investment strategy.

Moving from bonds into stocks, if you are looking for a safer way to purchase stock, then buying **equity funds** is a great way to spread out the risk. Instead of owning a single company's stock, you now partially own many companies' stock. This reduces the risk of one company failing and you losing all of your initial investment. The fund purchases hundreds of different companies, and you get a small piece of each when you invest in the fund. If the fund is something like an S&P 500 index fund, you buy "the stock market" in general. You don't necessarily have every stock on the market, but the S&P 500 contains 500 of the largest companies in North America.

Moving further up the risk scale, you also increase the risk when you look to purchase stocks from a company in a foreign country. Foreign stocks are riskier because it is a lot more complicated to get a good understanding of their business. They might try to deceive foreign investors and hide things to try and make the company seem better than it is. Foreign stocks are not very safe for beginners as you need to have a very in-depth knowledge of the market. The people living in the country will have a better idea of the rules and regulations that the company has to live by.

You can think of this by imagining the businesses in your own country. Even if you have not researched them, you will still have a good idea of the company's product, brand, customer base, management, owners, and current affairs compared to a foreign person. So a great way to decrease the risk of investing in foreign stocks is to invest in a foreign stocks fund. This again will limit the amount of research you will need to do on each company, and if one fails, you are hopefully covered by the performance of the other companies in the fund.

So passive investment options such as exchange-traded funds and index funds can be the passive investor's best friend. Sure, you won't get crazy 100X returns from investing in a broad index fund. Even if one company in the fund does become the next Amazon, you will only hold a small fraction of the shares in the company (depending on how much you invested in the fund).

But of course, on the other hand, if you invest in individual companies and one of them goes bust, you will lose a large part of your investment portfolio. If you were investing in a fund that tracks this company, it would only make up a small fraction of the entire fund.

GOALS AND TIME HORIZON

As we have already stressed in this book, your goals and risk combine to create your investment strategy. But timeframe also plays a massive role in what strategy you will take, and this means it will also be a factor to consider when we construct our portfolios. Let's say, for example, your investment goal is to save for a new car in 3 years. The timeframe on this goal would be considered medium term, so not too short and not too long. So our goal is to earn enough money from our investments to help purchase a new car, and the time frame is medium-term. As this goal is only a few years away, you would likely decide to put medium to low-risk assets into your portfolio.

But why? As we have learned, the stock market is ever-changing, and even if you invest in mutual funds, they can still take a long time to increase in value. It won't happen overnight, and within a 3-year time-line, the ETF or index fund you may have invested into could even be down money. Now, of course, some people will decide to say, "Forget this cautious approach. I am choosing risky assets. I want to buy a Tesla."

This, of course, would be your personal preference, and maybe you know something that the rest of us don't. But the likelihood is if you choose to fill your portfolio with risky assets like an ETF that tracks IPOs (initial public offerings when a company just becomes available to invest in publicly), you are likely to have less money in 3 years than you did when you started. So instead of a new Tesla, you might be able to afford a poster of the new roadster for your bedroom wall.

You see, there is an intricate dance we young investors must make between our investment strategy and the portfolio we create. Of course, we all want to reach our financial goals as soon as possible, but we must be sensible in our decision-making if we hope to make a profit.

As I said, the sooner you need the money from your investments, the more you should stick to safer assets. The **short-term** investments can earn you enough money to buy a P.C. or low-value item. If you save $100 a month, you will get to $600 in half a year. If you are saving for a holiday next year, the last thing you want to do is yolo all the money into a risky foreign start-up. You will miss out on the holiday because of poor investment planning. For this type of short-term goal, cash or a savings account at the bank can be a good option. But if you want to add a little risk, some of the safer bond funds options can be great.

Medium-term investing will have more ambitious goals. The goal with medium-term investments could be to earn enough to move out, buy a car or save for college. This might be a few years later, and getting decent returns will help you achieve your goals. Some higher yield bond funds or safer stock funds will help you get there within this timeframe. Let's say you can save $200 a month and need a car for college in 4 years. That $2,400 you saved the first year can turn into $2,700 or $2,900 with relatively low-risk investments.

That's several months' worth of savings "work-free." That's the beauty of investing; the people who do it right end up months ahead of those who don't. Sure, it takes a few years to see dramatic results, but the more time you have to hold your investments, the more you allow your money to compound. Soon you will have money growing and growing to the point you no longer need to work. In comparison, the poor individual who never learned how to invest will be working away until their retirement age.

POSSIBLE RETURNS AT DIFFERENT YIELDS

	Savings account (1% yield)	Bond (3% yield)	Low risk stock investment (5% yield)	High risk stock investment (12% yield)
Year 0	$2,400	$2,400	$2,400	$2,400
Year 1	$2,424	$2,472	$2,520	$2,688
Year 2	$2,448	$2,546	$2,646	$3,011
Year 3	$2,473	$2,623	$2,778	$3,372
Year 4	$2,497	$2,701	$2,917	$3,776

The table above illustrates this point excellently. Sure, the numbers are not groundbreaking, but over time and with consistency, you can turn your money into large riches. **Long-term investing** is for the future. Eventually, you know you will need money for things like starting a family, buying a house, or even saving for retirement. I realize these things are probably not first on your list of priorities, but if you currently have no financial goals or something in mind you are saving for, then planning for retirement is a great place to start.

Maybe you might like to plan on retiring early as I plan to do. My goal is to have the choice to retire at 40. Even if I did create enough wealth to do this, I'm not sure I would stop working, but having the option is always welcome.

Aside from saving for retirement, we can all agree that in today's world, too many people are struggling just to get by. As I have mentioned before, I can relate to those people. I still remember as a kid all those tough times my family and I went through. I believe that if enough young people get this high-quality information, we can turn the tide for many families in the future. Many millennials in their 30s are having trouble starting a family because they are stuck in small apartments and can't afford decent housing. I would love to see the next generation not repeat those mistakes.

Generally, as you are young, you can take a longer-term approach. Someone 45 years old will have a max of 20 years to grow their money before they need it to retire. Someone 15 years old can see their invest-ment account grow at least another 45 years. So the temporary ups and downs do not matter much.

The aim of this book is not to list every available asset on the market and tell you if it is low risk, high risk, short term, long term, or anything else in between. This information can easily be researched online and will depend heavily on what brokerage firm you decide to open your custodial account with (more to come on custodial accounts). We want to give you the tools to decide what portfolio will bring you the best results, and once you know what you want to build, you can then choose the assets that best fit your needs. All the passive investment options we mention throughout this book are a great place to start.

But please remember there is an index fund or ETF for just about anything you can imagine investing in, so we can't possibly cover them all here. We can, however, answer all the questions you may have regarding this book or how to use the information provided. Please always feel welcome to email the team directly at *admin@younginvestor-bob.com* or reach out on our Facebook group, *"Investing For Teenagers."* We can then provide further information that may help you on your journey.

CONSERVATIVE VS. AGGRESSIVE PORTFOLIO

So, what would you get if you choose a bunch of Treasury bond ETFs, combined with a high-interest savings account and a small fraction of your investment capital invested in a low-cost index that tracks the S&P 500? You would have a conservative portfolio. The assets I have mentioned above are low risk and then somewhat low risk as the S & P index would carry a little more risk than the others. But as we have a smaller fraction of our money invested into this index fund, this means most of our money is in very safe assets like government Treasury bonds, where we are guaranteed not to lose money on our investment.

Whereas let's say someone was to invest 90% of their money into riskier assets such as an ETF that tracks foreign stocks, an ETF for an emerging market (like Africa, for example), or perhaps an index that tracks something like the Russell 2000 (2,000 of the smallest companies in the U.S.). This would be considered an aggressive portfolio, as the person who might create this is willing to take on more risk in the hopes of higher rewards.

In the section above, I described how some assets are safer (less chance of the business failing) and less volatile (less intense ups and downs). Conservative portfolios are best for people with low-risk tolerances and a shorter time horizon. This is because they will need the money sooner or might panic if their portfolio's value decreases. A conservative portfolio might contain a lot of safe bonds and only stocks from large and well-established companies.

Aggressive portfolios are more suited to people with a high-risk tolerance and long time horizon. This allows for a higher average return but at the cost of higher volatility and more risk. For example, an aggressive portfolio might involve a stock-only approach. A portfolio with a lot of stock is risky enough as is. But if you want to take it a step further or add a little spice to a safer portfolio, you could include some smaller companies or start-ups with a new technology that is creating a lot of hype.

Just remember that a lot of the time, the hyped-up stocks will go on to fail, with the retail investor being the ones to lose out. To help you picture what returns are possible from different portfolios, let's look at some examples. Here are some of the returns and losses you can expect from different asset types (from data for the last 94 years) (Tepper, T. (2021, May 12))·

AVERAGE RETURNS FOR ASSET TYPE

	Average Returns	Worst Year
Bonds	6%	-8.1%
Stocks	10.2%	-43.1%
50% Stock + 50% Bonds	8.6%	-22.5%

In the long run, the return from stocks completely smoked bonds—6% vs. 10% can mean almost double your money if you wait long enough.

But when stocks lose money, they can do it in a very dramatic way. Please notice this data is for all stocks. If I had excluded the safer stocks, the worst year would probably be at -60% or -70%. Many individual technology stocks lost 80% or 90% of their value in the early 2000s, including good companies like Amazon and Google.

This was known as the tech bubble. Throughout history, many cases of bubbles have formed in the market. I mentioned above the housing crisis of 2008—that was a bubble. Then 8 years previous to this, the tech bubble popped. A bubble simply means the value of assets in a particular sector has become extremely overvalued. Every company will have its intrinsic value (the true value it is worth). Of course, this true value is very hard for investors to calculate. When times are good or perhaps a stock is gaining a lot of hype, a bubble can begin to form where people begin to speculate that the price of the stock or sector will never go down. Eventually, people realize that the price is massively overvalued and begin to sell their shares. This causes the price to drop dramatically, and the bubble "bursts".

Now bubbles are one thing, but often the market is down for reasons that have nothing to do with overvaluations. Often when times are tough, and money is tight, people panic and start selling off their assets.

Then when other people see the price going down, they also panic and begin to sell off their stocks. I know very few people willing to sit by while years of hard-earned money evaporates daily and do not panic. But people who don't panic and realize the markets have historically gone on to recover end up better off than those who panic and sell. So again, knowing your real risk tolerance is vital to picking the right balance between a conservative and an aggressive portfolio. The worst thing an investor can do is panic and sell at the lowest point. Due to this psychological pressure, many "buy high and sell low," ensuring they lose money from investing.

OTHER FACTORS THAT AFFECT A PORTFOLIO

Before we look at some portfolio examples, let's cover some other important aspects that can influence your portfolio.

Diversification

The first way to diversify a portfolio is to own a selection of assets across many different sectors and industries. A Sector simply means a group of companies that have a lot in common. Let's look at 3 companies, all in the oil industry. All of the companies drill for oil in different locations around the world. Even though they might be different companies with different locations, they are more similar than different and would fall into the "oil sector."

But what happens if the price of oil suddenly drops worldwide? Each oil drilling company's stock would take a hit, and if you solely focus on investing in the oil industry, you can be left exposed. If you want to pick stocks on your own, multiple studies have shown that to diversify a portfolio successfully; you should own a minimum of 20 individual stocks and sometimes up to 50 or more. So you see, creating a diverse portfolio by choosing individual stocks to buy is quite difficult. Plus, it can be very expensive.

For example, if you were to purchase a single share in every company currently in the S&P 500, it would cost you a small fortune. Another way is to own shares in all the companies is through index funds or ETFs (Exchange-Traded Funds).

As we know, these funds invest in tens or hundreds of different companies at once, and if you invest in the fund, you also get a piece of the pie. Some generalist funds reflect the whole stock markets, like the Dow Jones or the S&P 500. Some ETFs tend to be more focused on specific sectors, like tech ETFs or Chinese ETFs. ETFs have boomed in recent decades, so today, you can find one for almost anything. The best strategy for optimal diversification is to pick generalist funds or hold multiple forms of index funds or ETFs. However, picking 6 different ETFs, all specialized in tech, does not provide diversification because the idea of diversification is to provide you with protection against a downturn.

So if the tech sector crashed, all of your portfolios would be down as you were not diverse and too concentrated on tech funds. The second way to diversify a portfolio is to spread your capital between many different assets. For example, you could invest a large amount of your money in low-risk assets like Treasury bonds. Then mixing some more risk into your portfolio, you could choose a more volatile exchange-traded fund that tracks an emerging market. The hope with this method of diversification is again to protect you from potential downturns. If, for example, your ETF was down, you would be more protected as you hold stable government bonds.

Another advantage is that different asset prices can move in opposition to one another. For example, maybe stocks are going down, but bonds and gold are going up. So overall, the portfolio is doing fine even during the worst market conditions. Many people will often suggest a portfolio with a ratio of stocks to bonds that depends on your age.

For example, a younger investor would hold more stocks with only a fraction of their portfolio in bonds. This is because they generally have a higher risk tolerance and seek higher returns. Plus, they have the time to recover from a down market. But as you age, you soon realize you need to save for retirement. So you would begin to sell off some of your risky stock and buy safer bonds. The idea here is to protect you from losing all of your money just before you retire.

Also, don't worry if you are still unsure of stocks, bonds, index funds, ETFs, and all other assets you can invest in, as we will be covering them in more detail in the coming chapters.

Liquidity

A term you might encounter when reading about an asset is liquidity. This means the number of people buying and selling it daily. This can be important because it is useless for a price to go up if very few people are willing to buy it from you.

Government bonds or bonds of large corporations, along with stocks of large corporations, are very liquid. You will virtually always find a buyer and a seller. These are the most liquid assets just after cash itself. Think of the reasons why liquidity is important. You might need money one day, and if you have a large amount of money invested, if your asset is liquid, you can pull some or all of the money out—depending on the situation.

Illiquid assets can be collectibles, real estate, and private companies (not traded on the stock market). No matter the real value of these assets, finding a buyer can take a while and be a hassle. Maybe real estate prices are great in the neighborhood, but it is hard to find someone looking to buy a house there. Sure, it is great that the price of the house has risen in value, but if you can't sell at this time and the market later falls, you don't realize any potential gains.

Regarding stocks, low liquidity can be an advantage to individual investors. Very large banks and funds can only invest in very liquid companies. When they buy $1 billion worth of shares at a time, they need to find a lot of sellers at once. This also means many professional traders and analysts only look at large companies. This means that smaller companies can often be mispriced. But remember that smaller companies are also riskier, so keep an eye on your diversification. Perhaps an ETF that tracks small-cap companies (a company that is usually worth between 300 million to 2 billion) can offer the upside and protection from the risk that comes with the smaller companies.

PORTFOLIO EXAMPLES

Even though an investment portfolio is very personal, looking at the examples of some famous investors might help you find inspiration for your own. There are almost infinite ways to do it. Each portfolio mentions "bonds" or "stocks" in general, and for beginners, I recommend you first pick a fund that invests in many of these assets. Rather than picking individual stocks and bonds as choosing them individually is hard enough even for experienced investors.

The classical 60/40 portfolio

This is something advisors have recommended to investors for decades, 60% stocks and 40% bonds. The idea is that as bonds and stocks move opposite each other, the portfolio is more stable. Some variations exist, like tweaking down the percentage of bonds the younger you are. While this is not terrible, I think this doesn't work as well nowadays. Government bonds brought very low income in the last few years, so it can be a pretty low yield portfolio.

Ray Dalio's all-weather portfolio

Ray Dalio is the founder of the world's largest hedge fund. Think what you want of hedge funds, but their job is to manage investment risk daily. Dalio spent decades studying world economic history to find a safe and high-yield portfolio. Here's how it looks:

RAY DALIO'S ALL-WEATHER PORTFOLIO				
Long-term Bonds (10 years or more)	Short-term Bonds (2-10 years duration)	Stocks	Gold	Commodities
40%	15%	30%	7.5%	7.5%

A long-term bond with a maturity of 10 years means the holder of the bond will be paid back their money after 10 years. Over the 10 years, the person who purchased the bond will be paid interest at set intervals, such as every 6 months.

A commodity is a general term for everyday goods people purchase and interchange. Some examples include grain, oil, natural gas, and food. The large section of bonds provides a lot of stability to the portfolio. Stocks provide higher returns in periods of good economics. Gold and commodities provide results in periods of trouble and inflation. The all-weather portfolio has slightly lower returns than a 60/40 or the S&P 500 in most periods. But when a huge crash occurs, like the tech bubble of 2000 and the inflation of the 70s, it outperformed other portfolios. So over a very long time (20 years and more), it provides similar returns with a lot less volatility.

The permanent portfolio

The permanent portfolio was created by an investment analyst, Harry Browne, to be profitable in all possible economic conditions. So it is similar to Ray Dalio's idea but a bit simpler.

THE PERMANENT PORTFOLIO			
Long-term Bonds (10 years or more)	Stocks	Gold	Cash
25%	25%	25%	25%

Stocks and bonds provide yield, while gold protects against a crash or inflation. The cash part of this portfolio is what makes it unique because you rebalance the portfolio regularly (more to come on rebalancing in the next section). The cash is used to purchase the asset that may have reduced in value during a potential crash. For example, if stocks are down in value and you notice an opportunity to buy more of the funds you hold, we would use the cash to buy more and hope the price rises.

The ETF diversified portfolio

Diversification can mean many things. Ideally, you want different types of assets (stock, bonds, etc.) but also different economic sectors, geography, etc. This can be easily achieved using exchange-traded funds.

The best method is to choose options that tend to do the opposite of one another. This means if one asset is down, the other asset or assets should be up. A good portfolio should help reduce volatility without sacrificing too many returns. By focusing on a stock-only approach, you are still at risk of higher volatility in the case of a global recession.Here are some possible ETF-based portfolios:

Geography diversification

GEOGRAPHY DIVERSIFICATION		
U.S stock Market ETF	European stock Market ETF	Emerging Markets ETF
33.3%	33.3%	33.3%

Sector diversification

SECTOR DIVERSIFICATION				
Tech ETF	Energy ETF	Commodities ETF	REIT (real estate fund)	Consumable Goods ETF
20%	20%	20%	20%	20%

In geography and sector diversification, you simply input exchange-traded funds that suit the portfolio. Of course, you will still have to do some research and make sure the ETF is a good reputable fund with low fees and no-account minimums. But, you could create an infinite number of diversified portfolios using ETFs, as there is one for every asset type you can imagine.

Your own

The more experienced you become, the more you will have your ideas about investing.

Maybe you want to modify one of the examples and replace half of the gold with crypto or add farmlands, start-ups, or anything that interests you. Just remember, the investments that can produce the highest returns also have the highest risk. Alternatively, you can ask a human advisor or a Robo-advisor to build a portfolio fitting your needs.

MANAGING A PORTFOLIO

Once you have decided on your investment strategy and built a portfolio that is perfectly tailored to you, now you need to monitor your portfolio over time. This does not mean you must check your stock brokerage account 5 times a day. In fact, the less you think about your investments, the better off you will be. Of course, you will eventually have to recheck and reassess your investments, and it is recommended to do this every 6–12 months (C. (2021, April 11)).

If you obsess and check your portfolio too often, you will likely make a mistake one day when your investments are down and sell early. To avoid panic buying/selling, checking your portfolio every 6 months can be a good way to get a long-term feel for how things are going and what might need to be changed. When you look at your portfolio, I imagine the first thing you will want to know is how much money you made (for sure, this is what I do). But you should also check if the portfolio is still balanced. Let's look at the portfolio below:

REBALANCING		
U.S stock Market ETF	European stock Market ETF	Emerging Markets ETF
33.3%	33.3%	33.3%

When you invested your money a year ago, each category was 1/3 of the total. But since the U.S. stock market increased in value, the European stock markets went down a little, and emerging markets did okay.

Overall, you had a great year, and the whole portfolio made you good money. But the portfolio breakdown now looks like this:

REBALANCING		
U.S stock Market ETF	European stock Market ETF	Emerging Markets ETF
45%	25%	30%

You want to rebalance the portfolio to its original ratio to prevent a U.S. market downturn from hurting your overall returns. Then, on the other hand, if the European market were to do well the following year, you would miss out on all the action. Originally you started with a 33% breakdown of each investment. This would have been decided because it best suited your strategy, so you built your portfolio to fit your needs.

Over time, if you don't keep things in check, you can find yourself investing blindly without direction. So keep an eye on your investments, and if your goals or life situation changes, you can always go back and rebalance or change your portfolio to fit your new goals. So that's why we rebalance, but how do we rebalance a portfolio?

Take a look at the example above. To get the balance back to the original 33%, we need to sell some of the U.S. ETFs we hold and purchase a small amount of emerging markets ETFs and a larger amount of European stock market ETFs. The math is quite simple: you will know the value of your total investments by adding up all 3 ETF holdings and then dividing by 3 to get 33%. Now that you know how much of each investment you need to hold, you can simply sell the amount of the U.S. market until it is now the desired amount and share the rest between the two others until they match the U.S. ETF.

This is also why you don't need to maintain your portfolio too often. You pay a fee to the broker each time you buy or sell. And yes, this is true for the apps and brokers promising "no trading fees."

They just make money from your trading in a more complicated way. So you want to rebalance things only when they move enough to cause a major imbalance. In the previous example, I would not rebalance if the ratio had become just a 36%/30%/33%. Only once there are serious imbalances would I act on it.

I would say there is no perfect portfolio available today. It is a very subjective design process. Your goals will differ from mine, and my goals will vary from 90% of the world. So I would suggest not blindly picking a portfolio above and begin choosing assets that would fit that portfolio. Use the examples as templates, especially if you think some already closely fit your strategy.

But make sure to analyze the portfolio for yourself and see if it is something that will help you reach your financial goals while also taking risk and time into consideration. Then some other factors to consider would be asset allocation, diversification, and possible returns the portfolio can offer. Once you have designed your perfect portfolio, you need to purchase assets best suited to that portfolio. The next chapter is designed to help you find those assets in the stock market, and as this book is a passive investment guide, the options we cover will be passive investment assets.

6

INVESTING IN THE STOCK MARKET

*Y*ou should be ready to take action at this point in the book. You are beginning to develop your investment strategy, getting to know your risk profile, and have considered a portfolio you might feel comfortable with. Now we will discuss passive investment options in the stock market, and you will be happy to know these are the assets that will make you wealthy if used correctly.

THE STOCK MARKET

Stocks represent partial ownership of a company. Bonds are partial ownership of a debt. Early in the history of Europe, merchants trying to sell these assets would encounter the problem of finding a buyer. They traditionally used their social network to find an interested party, but this was slow and ineffective. Over time, merchants and money lenders in the financial centers like Venice, Belgium, and the Netherlands would organize stock markets—literally like markets, but instead of buying groceries, they would buy and sell businesses.

The Dutch East India company was among the first to use this new trading system because the travel to find spices in Asia was dangerous.

So traders preferred to split the risk between multiple ventures. No different from our advice on diversification. Nothing is ever entirely new. Interestingly enough, as soon as stock markets became a thing, rabid speculation appeared, notably the 1720 South Sea Bubble in England. This company was supposed to replicate the East India company's extraordinary success. Despite showing no profit and having no real business activity, speculators kept exchanging the South Sea company stocks at higher and higher prices (Beattie, A. (2022, March 14))·

And like today, even actual geniuses can act dumb out of greed. In particular, Sir Isaac Newton, the most prominent scientist of his time, bought stocks of the South Sea company early on. He was also "Master of the Royal Mint," or the man in charge of money for the whole kingdom. At first, it went very well. Newton doubled his money and sold quickly, making a profit of £7,000 (think something like $7 million today). And then, for months and months, the stock prices kept rising. The mania took over England's entire nobility and elite, with everybody but Newton making tons of money.

Unable to resist the temptation, he purchased more stock just a few weeks before the bubble popped. He lost up to £20,000—almost 2/3 of his wealth. The lesson here is that even the most intelligent man of his generation could fail at investing due to his poor judgment. You and I are not going to invent entirely new fields in science, so we should not assume we are smart enough to succeed without a good plan when even Newton could not.

Since then, stock markets have grown increasingly, becoming a central part of our economies. At first reserved for the richest merchants in big cities, investing in stock has become easier and easier with the right connections. Today, an app on your phone to connect with your broker is all you need. Stocks publicly traded have also become more and more numerous. So are the large diversity of funds, ETFs, and other instruments to help you diversify at a low cost (Hwang, I. (2022, March 7))·

Opening a custodial account

Unfortunately for aspiring teen investors, we can't simply open a brokerage account and begin investing. You will need a parent or a guardian to open a custodial account for you. The rules and regulations that each custodial account will have depend on what state or country you live in. You need to understand that such regulations have been created to protect you. Having a parent involved with your early investments protects you from scammers and poor investment decisions.

It also puts a lot of responsibility on the account provider (brokerage firm), making it a regulated activity that only authorized companies can offer. For the same reasons, a custodial account generally cannot be used to speculate on very risky assets like options and futures. But don't worry, it still leaves plenty of investing possibilities that I will explain in this chapter (FRANK, ADAM (n.d.) *Custodial accounts*)·

The money and assets in a custodial account belong to the *"beneficiary,"* meaning *you.* But the decisions will be made by the *"custodian"*— the parent or guardian who has opened the account. Please note that custodians cannot take money out of the account for themselves. The money there belongs to you permanently and can only be used for your needs. The role of the custodian is to help pick the investments and maintain the account. The money can be taken out *"for the use and benefit of the minor."*

This excludes everyday spending like food and shelter but can be used for things you need before adulthood. This account would not be an ideal saving account for college; more of a general savings and investing account. If you want to save for further education, look into a 529 account.

Here is the best way to approach opening a custodial account, but obviously, you should adapt it to yourself and your relationship with your parents. You should also take into account how your parents feel about investing. If they have some experience themselves, do not dismiss it and at least listen to what they have to say.

Firstly, you should educate yourself about stocks, investing, and brokerage accounts. This book and especially this chapter are a good start. This way, when you talk about investing with your parents, they will realize that you are serious and have already put in some effort. Then you should sit down with your parents and explain why you want them to open your investment account.

Tell them where the money will come from and what you plan to do with it. Consider if your parents have any experience with investing themselves—including negative experiences. Maybe they lost a lot of money in 2008 and will initially refuse as they wish to protect you. Or they have had one strategy in the past that was successful, and they don't want you to find your investment path. This is when what you learned in this book will come in handy. You can explain why you have chosen the investment strategy and portfolio and what factors have led to your decisions—what kind of return you expect from it, and what volatility you are ready to tolerate.

It would help if you also emphasized how this is a first step in becoming an adult and taking on more responsibility. This step will help you prepare for the future. You can also remind them how they will ultimately have control over the account until your maturity. But please remember that your parent or guardian knows your situation better than anybody else. If they refuse, they are doing so to protect your best interest. Don't worry if you can't open an account right now, use the first couple of chapters of this book to sharpen your mindset, earn tons of money and begin to save and manage money like a pro. Then continue learning and developing your knowledge because you will be ready to hit the investing world by storm when the time comes.

For the readers and listeners of this book outside of the United States, don't panic if you haven't heard of the term custodial account. They are often available in your country, but they might operate under a different name. The laws and regulations for your country may vary from place to place. Perhaps you can begin investing at 18, or you are limited to what investments you can hold.

The first step would be to research your nation's laws. Find out what steps you need to take, and once you understand the process, discuss the option with your parents, similar to the above mentioned approach.

Which custodial account?

If you managed to convince your parents or guardian to open an account, it is time to pick the right broker for you. Brokers are the people helping you to buy and sell stocks. You tell them what you want to buy, and they find someone ready to sell. They charge a fee for the service. They also hold the stock for you and keep you informed of any important news, like dividend distributions.

A dividend is a share of a company's profits that is given to stockholders at a set time each year. It can be quarterly, every 6 months, or yearly. Of course, with such a large number of shareholders, the dividend paid each time is quite small—especially when you only hold a few shares. I won't tell you the name of my broker or the name of the best custodial account. This is a very personal decision, and each person's best account will differ. I *will* tell you how to look for and analyze the options to find the right broker for you.

The absolute minimum is, of course, to check if they offer a custodial account, as not every brokerage firm will. The second thing to check is the account minimum. Some companies will be fine with an initial deposit of a few hundred bucks. Some will ask for thousands. If you want to get started with a limited amount of money, this can exclude a lot of otherwise good brokers. Don't panic, however, as plenty of custodial accounts have no account minimums, meaning you don't need to have any money to open an account.

The next thing to watch out for is the reputation of the company offering the account. The larger, the older, the most well-known the company is, the better. You also want to check if there are ongoing or past scandals about this company and if your country's financial authorities properly accredit them. This can easily be checked by looking at the reviews online that past investors have left.

Next, you should know what assets you want to invest in. If you want to trade in ETFs and stocks outside of the country, you need a broker offering that option. This might narrow down your choices. Also, check that they offer an IRA and other specialized accounts. Not every broker will offer a full range of assets in their custodial accounts, so if you have your heart set on one type of investment, make sure they offer this option.

Another important question is how do you want to invest? Do you want some help, like Robo-advisors? Then a broker with quality support will score a lot of points. If you want to do everything yourself, a quality interface and good research tools like advanced charts, news, etc., will be a plus. Look at your investment strategy and portfolio and ask if the services offered match your needs.

An extra nice-to-have service is fractional shares. One share of a company is subdivided into smaller, cheaper parts. This is great for companies with a very high stock price, such as a $3,200 share of Amazon (price as of writing this chapter). Normally, you could invest in Amazon only by incrementing one share at a time. With a fractional share, you can buy just 1/20 of an Amazon share at $160.

If the broker's services are adequate and look like a reputable company, it's time to look at the fees. Every broker will charge different fees. Sometimes it is a fixed flat fee of $X per trade. Sometimes X% of each transaction. Maybe both. There might be advisory fees, maintenance fees, annual service fees, etc. Considering you might not be starting with a lot of money, I recommend fees based on percentage instead of a fixed amount—0.5% of $100 is 50 cents. But $5 on any transaction will hurt if you have only a small amount of money, to begin with (Segal, T. (2021, December 7))·

Lower fees are better. Obvious, right? But I left this suggestion to the end because it should not be the main reason to pick a broker. Good services, more options, and a solid and reputable firm are worth a little more, in my opinion. As a young investor, it is recommended not to do a lot of trading anyway. So the less trading you do throughout the year, the more money you will likely save. So if you lose 0.5% of your money to fees every year, this will not have much of an impact throughout your investing journey.

RETIREMENT ACCOUNTS (IRA)

Traditional IRAs reduce your taxes today, while Roth IRAs reduce them in the future. For young people, taxes are extremely low as we usually tend to have low incomes. This can make a Roth IRA an extremely valuable investment account because if we pay a small amount of tax now and let our invested money compound in the account, this could become a small fortune by the time we retire.

However, it is worth knowing that with a Roth IRA, you can't withdraw a lot of the money without penalties until you reach 59 ½ years of age. Some exceptions exist, such as a first-time home purchase, college expenses, and starting a family. However, the account usually has a $10,000 limit on these withdrawals, so you may face penalties and taxes if you make nonqualified withdrawals or take out too much (Schwab Brokerage. (n.d.))·

Not all brokerage accounts offer custodial IRAs, so you might want to check that out when picking a broker. In addition to your contribution, other people can also contribute to an IRA. So maybe a grandmother or an aunt can use it as a gift to you on special occasions. If you are going to make contributions to your account, it is important to know that it has to be earned income—so you will need a job, and the IRS will need to tax the money.

For someone opening this account, the goal is to save for retirement. IRAs are supercharged when you start early. For example, a $6,000 contribution at 15 years old will turn into $176,000 at 65 years old (assuming 7% average returns). To reach the same retirement money starting at 35 years old, you need to invest $23,000 or almost x4 more. This is how powerful early investing can be. One last type of investment account I did not mention is the 401(k). This is because it is usually accessible only to older people with stable full-time jobs. This is an account where employees can put a part of their salary toward a 401(k) plan, and the employer also adds some extra money. Like IRAs, there is a traditional 401(k) and Roth 401(k)—the difference being that, again, the Roth 401(k) is an after-tax retirement account.

We won't discuss this option so much as a 401(k) is usually only offered to a person in a full-time job, which might not be accessible to the average young investor. Of course, if you are currently working a full-time job, then by all means ask if your employer provides a 401(k) and if they are matching contributions, make sure to use this option as it is basically free money.

INDEX FUNDS

Now we will begin discussing some of the more popular passive investment options for people of all ages. Think of your custodial account as a way to invest your money. Then your retirement account is a protective wrapper you can put around the money in your account to protect it from taxes. What we discuss from this point onward are the assets someone can invest their money in. Think of an index fund as a pool of many different investors' money put together to buy multiple stocks instead of just one company. An index simply means a measure of something. So an index fund is trying to measure or closely match a specific financial market.

There are many different financial markets, so there are many different index funds to track those markets. Let's look at some of the most popular examples of index funds. The S&P 500 index tracks the stocks of the largest 500 companies in the USA. The Dow Jones Industrial Average (DJIA) index tracks 30 large U.S. industrial companies. The Nasdaq 100 index follows the top tech companies in the U.S. The FT Wilshire 5000 (FTW5000) index follows thousands of companies, trying to represent the whole market and not just the largest companies.

So what does it mean to track 500 of the largest companies in America, and how can we use this to make money? So a fund providing an index that tracks the S&P 500 will take the money you and others have invested and purchase the list of companies in that index. The aim of this fund is then to exactly match the returns of the 500 companies on that list.

The average return of the S&P 500 over the last 20 years has been 7.45%. So the fund tracking these 500 companies aims to provide those returns for its investors. Or get as close as possible (Lake, R. (2022, March 30))·

It is important to distinguish index funds from mutual funds. Mutual funds are large funds gathering the money of thousands of investors *actively invested* by the fund manager. This can be beneficial if the manager is highly skilled and disastrous if the manager performs poorly. Index funds are *passive*. They replicate the value of the stocks of the companies included in the index. The only decision taken is adding or removing companies from the index. So the returns from investing in index funds depend on the stock market performance, not the manager's skills. The other difference is that active funds tend to charge heavy fees, sometimes up to 1.5%. If the mutual fund you invested in returned 6% this year, a quarter of your profit went into the manager's paycheck. But, passive index funds have fees of just 0.2% (which can be even lower), barely noticeable in comparison.

When you compare the passively managed index fund to the performance of the actively managed mutual funds, the passive index funds beat the majority of actively managed funds. Partially this is due to the fees I mentioned. But also because it is very hard to beat the market. Consistently choosing stocks over a long period of time that outperform the market is very, very difficult.

That is why most actively managed funds fail to outperform passively managed funds. A 2015 study revealed that only 25% of actively managed funds outperformed their benchmark, slightly up from 2014 when 18% of active managers outperformed the benchmark (Hassine, M. (2016))·

Indexes are very diverse, so they experience fewer ups and downs because they contain roughly the same companies over time. They also cost a lot less in trading fees as they buy and sell less often. Another bonus of the index fund is the lower taxes compared to active funds.

This is because every time an investor or the manager of a fund has to buy or sell assets, they will firstly be taxed on any capital gains they might have made (profit), and then they will have to pay trade fees on top of that.

Overall, index funds are a good way to start investing. They offer diversification with low fees and don't require much knowledge to get started. Once you have more experience and practice with investing, you can decide if you want to try something else, like mutual funds or individual stock picking.

One limitation is that many index funds ask for a minimum investment of up to $1,000. So other options are better if you are starting with limited cash. However, if the idea of an index fund sounds good to you and you can't reach the account minimum above, don't worry. Some brokerages offer index funds with no account minimums (Johnston, M. (2022))·

In any case, remember that index funds are 100% stocks. So refer to your investment strategy to see how much stock you are willing to hold in your portfolio. Even though they are very diversified and have many advantages to the young investor, there is risk involved with stock market investing, so do your research beforehand.

Index fund examples

There is no shortage of index funds available on the market today, and for us to list each option would be counterproductive. But to give you a good starting point for researching some that might suit you, we will list some of the most popular options on the market and what they track. Please understand that we are not suggesting you invest in any of these index funds. We are listing them here for education and to help you understand the options.

Market Cap Indexes

A small-cap stock is anything valued between 300 million and 2 billion dollars. A lot of these companies would primarily do business in the United States (or whatever country they originate from), and they would not yet have cracked the international market.

These stocks are seen as very risky options due to how sensitive they are to the economic climate. If a recession were to hit, they would be the first to feel it, and many might lack the resources to stay afloat. Contrast this to mid-cap or large-cap companies, where they are much more stable and can ride out of tough economic times. However, small-cap funds also tend to have the highest room for growth, as the companies are smaller, and if they become mid- or large-cap, the shareholders could benefit massively. This leads to the characteristic high returns of small-cap funds and the extreme volatility they experience.

Gary Lemon, an economics professor at DePauw University, says that over a long period of 20 years, small-cap companies can outperform large-cap by quite a margin. Let's say you invested $10,000 in both a large and a small-cap fund. With the historical rates of return for both funds, you could expect to earn $63,700 from the large and $100,000 from the small funds—that is 36.3% more money!

So great, why don't we just put all of our money into small-cap funds? Well, if you don't wait for a long enough period, the volatility can mean you lose a massive amount of your investment.

For example, in 2008, you could have lost 36.1% of the value in small-cap stocks (Chang, E. (2019, July 26)). An example of a small-cap index would be the Russell 2000 (U.S. news money).

Moving up from small to mid-cap, these funds would try and track a particular index of mid-cap stocks. A mid-cap company would be valued between 2 billion–10 billion. The positive about a mid-cap company is it has passed the early years of doing business, where approximately 30% of new businesses fail, 2 years into operating (something to keep in mind if you want to invest in small-cap funds). Worse still, 45% fail within 5 years and 65% within the first 10 years (U.S. Bureau of Labor Statistics. (2016, April 28))· One benefit of investing in mid-cap funds is if small caps tend to be performing well over a certain period, or on the other hand, large caps seem to be performing well. Investing in a middle ground ensures you will benefit from either market situation.

Finally, let's discuss large-cap index funds. These funds are companies with a market capitalization of 10 billion or more. Imagine today's business giants like Coca-Cola, Disney, or Apple, for example. These companies not only tend to have a large market cap, but for the most part, they have an excellent history of doing business and are much more secure than the small or mid-cap companies.

This extra security brings a massive risk reduction, but as we have learned, a risk reduction also means a reduction in possible returns. As the companies are already so large, it can be difficult to continue to increase production and find new customers.

People like to use these funds as they often pay dividends (a share of the profits to stockholders), and this can be a great method of having continued passive income roll in. These dividend payments can some-what counteract the lower rates of growth that the companies will likely have.

Bond Index Funds

Now that we have covered a stock example let's discuss bond index funds. This is a broad example as you can technically have many different bonds in the fund.

For example, this index fund could track U.S. Treasury securities, U.S. Savings bonds, Corporate bonds, and international bonds—to name a few. Of course, what fund you choose will depend on your investing strategy.

If you are happy to receive fewer returns in exchange for safety, maybe a U.S. Treasury index fund would suit you best. Whereas if you wanted more rewards and were willing to take more risk, then maybe an index of international or emerging market bonds would be a good fit. Bond index funds can be a great way to diversify a portfolio and bring some stability. However, you won't get wealthy from this type of investing. Bonds are much better suited to someone who has already made a good living and is now beginning to set up for retirement. We young investors are looking to grow our wealth, so we need to take a little more risk with our investments. But of course, the option is there for you and if an index that tracks a bond market sounds right for you, then go for it (Kenny, T. (2022, March 1))·

One important thing to remember about bonds and stocks is that they usually tend to perform in opposite directions. If stocks are down one year, it is a good bet that bonds will likely be up. Outside of some of the more technical reasons like interest rates, an easier answer can simply be that both assets are fighting for investors' capital. If many people invest in the stock market, there is less money in the bond market, which will lower the price. So if you are looking to be more cautious and have a more diverse portfolio, maybe you would like to hold a certain amount of your portfolio in stocks and some in bonds.

International Index Funds

An international index fund aims to track the performance of an international market. For example, some of the most popular and well-established international indexes would track the European, Japanese, or even Chinese markets. Often a fund will combine a list of international markets into an index. So the European market might make up 50% of the index fund while the other 50% is broken down into China, Japan, and some emerging markets.

These international funds can be extremely volatile depending on the market it tracks. The risk with international stock is also different from the normal business risk. You may also have to deal with currency issues, government corruption, liquidity issues, and less regulation than the United States. If you are not a massive risk taker and are not trying to find the next great worldwide economic superpower, I would be cautious with too much international exposure in your portfolio.

Sure it is a good method of benefiting from a market without the risk of individually buying these foreign businesses. But when you look at an international index fund such as the one offered by Vanguard (this is a brokerage firm) called the Total International Stock Index Fund Admiral Shares (VTIAX), this fund's performance over the past 10 years has been 5.80%. The fund tracks markets such as Europe, the Pacific, the Middle East, North America, and emerging markets (Blokhin,

A. (2022, April 25))·

When you consider the performance of something closer to home like the S&P 500 index, with an average 10-year return of 13.6% (Knueven, L. (2021, June 14)), why would you take the extra risk of going abroad when the performance at home has been so promising. Now, of course, that doesn't paint the whole picture, and the market performance can change at the drop of a hat. But keep these things in mind when you are constructing your portfolio. Why take the extra risk if the chance of high rewards is not obvious?

Above, we have listed three examples of index funds. But in reality, we could have chosen many different options, and better and worse index funds are available than the ones we have listed.

One important thing to understand here is that a market-cap index tracks companies depending on their size. But you can't invest directly in a market-cap index without a brokerage firm's help and the fund they provide. Each brokerage firm will have its unique version of the index fund. If you want to track something like a broad market index (like the S&P 500), you will first have to decide what brokerage firms index you would like to invest in.

As a teen investor, this also might be limited to the one offered by your custodial account. But still, once you have your full investing account when you mature, this is important to understand. Below is a list of some of the top S&P 500 index funds offered by different brokerage firms:

- Fidelity 500 Index Fund (FXAIX)
- Schwab S&P 500 Index Fund (SWPPX)
- Vanguard 500 Index Fund Admiral Shares (VFIAX)
- State Street S&P 500 Index Fund Class N (SVSPX)
- SPDR S&P 500 ETF (SPY)

Is one a better option than another? Maybe, but you will have to determine if you are looking for performance, low-cost, no-account minimums, low yearly expense ratio, no commission, reputation, and all other important factors. And the same is true for every index fund you might like to invest in. Each broker will likely offer their version or variation of the index, so you must decide what works best for your goals.

ETF

ETF stands for exchange-traded funds. It is a fund generally focused on one type of company or sector. They are new financial instruments that only started in 1993, with more than 2,000 different ETFs existing today. What makes ETFs special is that they can be bought or sold like a stock throughout the day. And rather than simply purchasing every company stock that the ETF holds, you can own a fraction of each company by investing in the fund.

The ability to buy and sell ETFs throughout the day is one of the major differences between them and index funds, as index funds can only be purchased or sold for a set price at the end of the trading day (Davis, C. (2022, March 16))·

ETFs are very similar to index funds. Imagine you want to invest in a lot of "growth" stocks and the advantages a growth market can bring, but you don't want to take the higher risk involved in buying single-growth companies.

So to get some diversification and hope to benefit from the overall positive trend of a growth sector, you would buy an ETF that focuses on growth companies. What distinguishes a growth company from another company is its ability to create and sustain above-average earnings or cash flow.

Typically, a growth company will hope to increase the overall size of its business rapidly by reinvesting its profits. Generally, a growth company will appear expensive, trading at a high price-to-earnings ratio (don't worry about this ratio, this will be covered in Part 2 of the series along with more on growth stocks). But in reality, if the company continued to grow at its current rate, it could be relatively cheap. So people often speculate on growth stocks; they purchase the stock in the hope of higher returns further down the company's lifecycle. Of course, this type of investing can provide some of the best results. But they also carry massive risk, as investors are paying above-average prices for companies they "hope" to grow in the future (Hayes, A. (2022, February 8))·

ETFs are a great way to invest in a specific idea or sector while also being diversified. Maybe you want to invest in biotech, renewable energy, or Chinese companies. Instead of picking individual companies in the sector, you can buy an ETF containing at least the most important stocks within that particular sector (Merrill Edge. (n.d.))·

Nowadays, there is virtually an ETF for everything. If you want to invest in the Asian continent, excluding the Japanese market, there is an ETF for that. If you want to invest in biotech companies focusing on genomics, sure, there is one for that. In electronic chips makers, car makers, undervalued companies, or dividend-paying companies—no matter the investing idea, there is an ETF for it. The diversity that ETFs offer can be extremely beneficial to the young investor.

As mentioned before, investing in something we either have prior knowledge of or are interested in is always a good start. If you have a particular advantage in a sector or industry, maybe there is an ETF that invests in the sector for you. This will limit the need for you to do a lot of heavy research and offer you great diversification.

In the section above, I have just mentioned that some index funds can be out of the young investor's price range. Well, with ETFs, this usually isn't a problem. For example, some ETFs track the S&P 500 like an index fund. Both funds aim to track the index, but their approach differs slightly. For example, ETFs trade throughout the day (like stocks), whereas index funds can only be purchased or sold once at the market close. Another difference between the two is price. Index ETFs tend to be cheaper if you buy them commission-free (Hicks, C. (2021, February 1))·

You can also purchase an ETF that contains only bonds, which can be a good method of adding bonds to a portfolio. Many active and passive investors use ETFs to help create their ideal portfolios—as they are very adaptable. If you notice your portfolio is weak in a certain area and need an adjustable asset type to fill a gap, then ETFs can be your best friend.

The majority of ETFs are passive. They list the companies they want to track and replicate the price movements. In contrast, a special type of ETF is an actively managed ETF. These ETFs are much closer to mutual funds as a manager frequently decides what to include and exclude from the ETF. The advantage over mutual funds is normally cheaper fees and no account minimums, meaning no minimum buy-in.

Examples of ETFs

Value

Part 2 of this book series will develop our understanding of how to research and invest in individual companies. There are many different methods and strategies to follow. But three popular methods are growth, dividend, and value investing. Each investing type has characteristics and metrics that point to what category a company might fit into.

For example, a company trading at a low price-to-earnings ratio or low price-to-book (again, these ratios and how to calculate them will be discussed in the next part of this series) could be considered a value company. A great way to imagine a value company is to think of a sale at the local electronics store. One week ago, a customer purchased a television for full price, say $500. Then only one week later, the store puts a massive 50% discount on all items. Now you walk in and buy the same T.V. for $250. The same can be true for stocks. For different economic reasons and market conditions, companies often fall out of favor with the general public.

When the stock is being overlooked by the majority of investors, it is trading at a price that is lower than its intrinsic value (the true fair value of the company). So you purchase a stock worth $50 a share for the price of $25. The hope of value investing is then for the stock price to rise back to its fair market price of $50, allowing you to pocket $25 per share (Graham, B. (2003)).

Generally, these stocks tend to be low risk as you put a "margin of safety" on your investment. Even if you have miscalculated the company's intrinsic value and it is only worth $25, you stand to lose little to no money. Even though this style of investing is relatively low risk, you can still benefit from an ETF that tracks a group of value stocks.

The major advantage is avoiding the long and laborious process of researching and calculating if a company is truly a value stock. Not only is this time-consuming, but you also stand to make some errors in your calculation, especially if you are new to the process.

So instead, you can put your money in the hands of a professional and allow them to pick a bunch of value stocks for you. So this type of fund would be ideal for a conservative portfolio, as it can outperform growth funds during volatile markets. However, in bull markets, they can produce fewer returns, as growth stocks can benefit from the bull rush.

Dividend

Another popular method of investing in stocks is to find ones that consistently pay dividends. The idea of dividend investing is to benefit not only from any potential growth a company might experience but also from the regular dividend payments it distributes to its customers. This means you get passive income from your investment and can potentially receive a capital gain if you decide to sell the stock.

Once again, this ETF can offer protection from any potential downturn in a sector, as dividend ETFs can hold anything from 50 to 100 companies in the fund. Of course, with this decrease in risk and broader diversification, there is a drawback. When investing in dividends, the amount the company pays you regularly is called the dividend yield. In other words, the dividends paid annually are divided by the current share price. Obviously, the larger the dividend yield, the better, as you will receive more money from your investment (be wary, though, as a high dividend yield can sometimes indicate that a company is failing). But as the dividend ETFs are so broad, you will likely get a more average dividend yield when compared to choosing your own dividend stocks (Segal, T. (2022, February 9)).

Again, the ETF options above are simply for your learning. There are endless amounts of ETFs available on the market today. The key here is to understand what the funds can offer you—good diversification, lower risk, less research, saves time, good introduction for a beginner, and the performance over a long period of can be better than active investing (for most people).

But if any of the investing methods above stands out to you, maybe they would be a good place to begin your research. If you like the idea of a more conservative approach to the stocks you hold in your portfolio, maybe an ETF that tracks value funds could be right for you. If you are looking to add some risk and aim for larger rewards, then maybe you would like to choose a sector ETF that tracks the technology industry, as this is usually full of growth companies and has historically given the highest possible returns. But, of course, remember the 2000 tech bubble where they all lost a massive portion of their value. Even amazing companies like Amazon lost nearly 90% of their value during the bubble (Davis, A. (2018, December 18), so all things must be considered before putting our money into any investment option.

Which one?

If you were wondering what is best, an index fund or ETF, it's best not to think of it this way. They are both great passive investing options for the young investor. Refer back to your investment strategy and understand how much stock-based assets you would like to hold. If you are a beginner, an index fund or an ETF tracking an index is probably the best way to get started.

Also, I know many of the concepts and information throughout the book are self-learned and self-developed. But don't worry, in this book's final chapter, we will give our opinion on the best course of action you can take to start making money.

What is the right fund for me?

I know that the diversity of choice can be a bit overwhelming. But you don't need to invest in every option shown in this chapter. You don't even need to learn about each of them. My goal is to give you a starting point and the knowledge to make your own decisions. If you need to ask follow-up questions, you can email The Young Investor team directly (admin@younginvestorbob.com) or reach out on Facebook (Facebook group: Investing for Teenagers). Of course, you also need to understand the disadvantages of index funds, ETFs, and passive investing, so let's briefly discuss the drawbacks.

Disadvantages of passive investing

There is no perfect investing strategy. One may perform better or worse than another during certain economic conditions. But unfortunately, there is no one-size-fits-all strategy, which will largely depend on your personal preference. Throughout this book, and especially in this chapter, we have highlighted the positives of passive investing. Of course, it does tend to outperform active (in most cases), as we have seen, and it is a great way for a young investor to get started.

But as with everything in life, there are some drawbacks to the strategy. You will not "beat the market" with passive investing. The goal is to track a particular index, like the S&P 500. No matter what the economy is doing, whether up or down, you will receive average results—as that is the strategy's aim. Also, if you are tracking a particular index, in this example, let's use the Russell 2000. This means you blindly invest in thousands of companies without any due diligence or research.

This can become an issue if one company makes up most of the fund (not every company will have the same weighting in the fund). If a poorly performing company makes up a large portion of the fund, you can stand to make some large losses. If it were an actively managed fund, perhaps the fund manager could have seen the red flags with the company.

You cannot react to market conditions with passive investing, whether in an index or ETFs. For example, if something catastrophic were to happen in the market, the fund would continue to track its index and hold the same companies, no matter what. It cannot sell some of the assets in the fund and try to find better options that might suit the current market. This lack of management provides lower fees and cheaper investing for you and me. But it can also leave you looking at the next field, which has much greener grass (Snelling, D. (2020, November 3)).

Summary

To start investing, you will need to open a custodial account. This means finding a reliable broker to open the account with. It will also involve getting your parents or guardian on board with the idea. Once this is done, you can start investing. A beginner-friendly option is index funds, giving you exposure to "the market." In the long run, this will bear good results with the minimum effort. If you want to pursue a more determined strategy, you can start looking for an ETF that fits your needs.

If you want to do it yourself, you will need to learn more about picking individual bonds and stocks, which is for the next book in this series! The final chapter of this book will be an investing outline that a typical young investor can take to start making money. We will be giving a simple description of a method any teen investor can take to increase their wealth.

We understand that many of this book's concepts may have been hard to understand fully. But fear not; we will highlight the important points again and provide you with an easy-to-use investing guide in the books final chapter.

7

THE YOUNG INVESTOR
APPROACH

*A*t this point in the book, it is normal to feel enthusiastic and confused. But let me assure you, investing is something you can succeed at with proper dedication. Of course, you will not become a pro by reading one investing book, but this is a good start, and we at The Young Investor have many more resources to help you improve your skills.

I understand that the information in this book may have been a little technical at times, which may have caused some confusion. To combat this, the final chapter of this book will be a quick summary of the important points we have covered, and we will also provide you with an example of a strategy that could work for the average teen investor. Remember that this is just our opinion. We base this opinion on our own personal knowledge and the most up-to-date information available to us. Feel free to disagree and tweak this approach to your needs. The idea is that you can use this approach as a template to modify instead of having to figure it all out from scratch.

Investment Strategy

Before we jump into an example of an investing strategy that might work for the average teenager, we need to cover several key points.

First, don't skip ahead and begin investing without an emergency fund. Trust me; you are shooting yourself in the foot if you begin investing without having some money saved up in case of an emergency. Let's face it; there will always be some situation where you need cash, so experts recommend keeping at least 3–6 months of your income saved for a rainy day. Without this extra protection, you can be blindsided when you need a couple of hundred bucks. Suddenly, you need to sell off your investments to cover this life expense; trust me, this is counterproductive.

Also, for one reason or another, you could find yourself in debt in the future. Perhaps you need to take out a loan for a new car or other living expenses. If this is a high-interest loan, and you need to pay back your money plus a large interest, it is advised that instead of continuing to invest your money in the market, you should stop and focus on clearing the debt. Continuing to invest may seem like the smart thing to do as we try to earn more money to help clear the debt. But over time, we will lose more than we make, as it is difficult to outpace high interest.

If, for example, the loan's interest was 15%, you would have to make at least 15% from your investments to match the loan interest payments (considering both the value of the loan and the initial investment match). But when you consider the average return of the stock market is about 10% per year, you will struggle to get close to the amount needed. Of course, you could put more money into the market in the hopes that a 10% return on your investment would be enough. But, if we could invest more than the value of our loan, we likely wouldn't have taken the loan in the first place.

Investment goals

Of course, I can't create financial or life goals for you. This is a personal decision; everyone's situation and ideal life will be different. Don't fall victim to wanting an excessive lifestyle, where you buy new clothes each week and a new car every year. If you create modest financial and investment goals, you are more likely to achieve them and go on to create new investment goals.

You are better off hitting small manageable goals rather than having one goal of earning 10 million from your investments. Ask yourself why you have begun investing? Use these reasons as your driving force to keep going when times are tough. But also look at those reasons and see what clues they can give you to form your investment strategy. Are those goals going to be hard to achieve? This could mean you will have to take a more high-risk approach. When do you want to achieve the goals? Unless you are saving for something you will need in the next couple of years, then maybe a long-term approach is something that would work for you.

Write down all your goals in life and your investing goals, then use them to map out your investing strategy. Remember, your investment strategy should be personal to you. If you try to copy the style of another investor, it might cause undue stress as it doesn't suit your needs. Also, please realize that over time things can change, and if you realize your strategy is no longer working for you, it can be changed by repeating the initial design process.

Time frame

The strategy that stands out for the young investor in relation to a timeline is a long-term investment strategy. This strategy works so well for the teen investor because we have such a long time from initial investment to when we might need the money again (retirement). The best long-term assets would be things like stocks, as they might have a lot of volatility over the short term. But generally, the risk can be decreased if the assets are given enough time. Assets like stocks are also great over longer timelines as they offer the possibility of higher returns.

Of course, simply investing in a single company and waiting 10 years for the price to rise is not a good idea (not unless you have done proper research on the company). Especially when we are talking about passive investing, simply using an index fund or ETF that holds stock is a great way to reduce the risk over a longer timeframe. We also need to discuss another helpful strategy that can increase our chance of investing success massively: **Dollar Cost Averaging.**

Dollar-Cost Averaging

Dollar-cost averaging is an investment strategy that aims to reduce volatility by spreading your invested capital over a longer period rather than investing it all in one go. The easiest way to describe dollar-cost averaging is to imagine you have $5,000. You can invest it all into a low-cost index fund that tracks the S&P 500 today, or you can invest $500 into the fund over the next 10 weeks.

But what difference would that make, you might ask? Dollar-cost averaging is often compared to another purchasing method: "timing the market." Timing the market involves trying to purchase the asset when it is at its lowest point and then selling it once it reaches its high. In theory, this sounds great because you will maximize your profits if you buy low and sell high.

But the reality is nobody can pinpoint when a stock will reach a low or a high point. Often most experts don't even know what moves a stock will make tomorrow. So the idea with dollar-cost averaging is to reduce the risk of putting all your money into the market when the stock is trading at a high point. If you constantly put the same amount of money into the fund each month, this ensures that when the fund is trading at a higher price, you will buy fewer shares, and in the months when the price is lower, you will purchase more shares.

The hope with dollar-cost averaging (especially combined with a long-time horizon) is to reduce the volatility of the funds we invest in. It also aims to take emotion out of our investing decisions. Removing emotion can be one of the best things we can do for our investments. If we listen to our hearts too often and jump on a few overhyped stocks, we could lose a lot of our money and be left wondering if investing is really for us. Finally, we hope to reduce market mistiming. And as I mentioned above, even professional analysts can't perfectly time the market. So to give us young investors the best chance we have with investing, maybe we should consider employing a dollar-cost averaging approach to our investing strategy (Hayes, A. (2022, March 21)).

Risk

Going back to risk, the younger you are, the more time you have to recover from a mistake. Losing a lot of your wealth at 60 can be devastating. Losing 50% of the money you received from doing yard work at 17 is not such a big deal. For the young investor, a higher-risk strategy would probably be the best path forward. Again, we have so many years and decades to recover from sudden downturns. This would also vary depending on whether you are actively or passively investing. Being a little riskier when investing your money in an ETF that tracks growth stocks is still safer than actively investing your money in individual growth companies. True, you could put that money into safer, more stable large-cap companies like Alphabet, Amazon, Apple, or Coca-Cola.

But if you were also trying to find growth companies and you were investing 35% of your capital in one company, imagine if this company went bankrupt, you would immediately lose 35% of your net worth. However, the same is not true for ETFs or index funds, as the performance of the other companies in the funds would cushion the blow from one or two poor performers.

So with a longer timeline and diverse investment funds like index funds or ETFs, you may aim for assets that can produce higher returns. That said, please realize that investing purely in something like a growth ETF would not be wise. A somewhat risky investment that can bring good returns over time could be something as simple as an index that tracks a broad market (S&P 500, Russell 2000, or insert any broad market index you like here). All stock investments carry a certain level of risk, so when I state that you might like to take more risk in your strategy, this simply means being willing to hold more stock assets in your portfolio.

You don't need to invest in IPOs (these initial public offerings are seen as very risky investments) to satisfy the risk level suited to a young investor. Remember, the goal with your investment strategy is to take the amount of risk that will bring you to your goals as quickly as possible while allowing you to sleep at night.

In reality, if you could attain a 7% annual return over your investing career (which is very achievable), you would end up being a very rich man or woman once you reach your golden years.

So don't feel the need to take unnecessary risks where the possible rewards are not worth it. Most young investors like to take more risks in their strategy because they are trying to build wealth. If you were to compare our strategy to that of someone who is 60, then perhaps bonds would be enough for them as they are trying to maintain their wealth. In comparison, we are in the building phase of our careers. We need assets that produce significant returns over years and decades and turn our capital into thousands and hundreds of thousands. So in closing, more risk simply means being willing to hold more stock in your portfolio. It doesn't have to be the riskiest stock on the market.

Stay smart about taxes.

Taxes will chip away at your money for the rest of your life, so best make peace with that fact. That does not mean you cannot be smart about it. I am not a tax advisor, and you should talk to your parents about it. But remember that there are options to reduce taxes from your investing activities: Roth IRA, 529 plans, etc. Also, remember that the longer you hold an investment before selling it, the lower your taxes should be. This is one of the many advantages investors have over traders/speculators.

Investment Portfolio

Getting help?

Regarding the exact portfolio you will build, the first question is asking if you want help to build one. The task can feel overwhelming, and copying an existing portfolio or using advisors is fine.

Robo-Advisor

I have mentioned above that a Robo-advisor is an algorithm-based software that many brokerage firms now use to help people create an investing portfolio.

They usually work by asking a set of psychographic questions (study of human traits) and demographic (study of human population, by region, language, education, ethnicity, ETC.) to build a user model. The questions can be as basic as your location, gender, risk profile, or financial goals.

On the other hand, more complex Robo-advisors can monitor your financial habits, like your income and spending, to get a true measure of your financial behavior and gauge how you might react to specific market conditions. The problem with less complex Robo-advisors is that the questions and analyses they use are quite broad, and one person will receive very similar results to thousands of others.

This means you, your neighbor, and all your pals at football could technically be given the same investing advice on how to construct a portfolio. In truth, this doesn't have to be such a bad thing. Perhaps we can all make money together. But when you realize the best investors around the world (like Buffet) have made the majority of their money doing exactly the opposite of what the crowd was, then perhaps if we desire better than average results, we might have to do something a little different.

Thankfully, this problem can be solved by paying a higher fee. Suppose you pay for a Robo-advisor that uses artificial intelligence and machine learning. In that case, this tool can give you unique and comprehensive advice on how to construct and maintain your portfolio over the years (Ganatra, M. (2022, March 29)). Of course, these more comprehensive Robo-advisors will cost you. The top-of-the-line models can charge you up to 0.90% of assets under management (this is just slightly lower than some human advisors charge). Compare this to the simpler models, and you may only have to pay 0.25% (Henricks, M. (2022, February 9)).

So quite a large difference in fees. Perhaps the high fee models might be out of the young investor's price range. But of course, you are free to decide what works best for you. I included the breakdown of Robo-advisors here as they can be a great tool for the young investor.

Especially when we begin our journey, it can be helpful to have someone or something help us with building our first portfolio or deciding what strategy might work best for us. But in reality, you don't need to use any of these tools. With the help of this book and the free resources we provide, constructing your winning formula alone is very manageable. So for those who will do it alone, let's recap the key points of your investment portfolio.

Asset allocation

As I said, when you're young, you have little money to lose and plenty of time to learn and correct mistakes. That said, perhaps a more aggressive portfolio would better suit the young investor. This can be a high percentage of stock in the portfolio, or maybe even only stocks. The type of stock matters too. To achieve excellent long-term results, you don't necessarily have to invest in extremely risky assets. Assets such as medium to large-cap companies, value companies, and domestic companies can produce excellent results while minimizing risk.

Still, you must go back to your strategy and understand the risk you are ready to tolerate. Only go as far as you feel comfortable, and probably still dial down a notch from there. It is human nature to overestimate our risk tolerance until problems arise. So, in this case, it is better to be slightly less aggressive than slightly too aggressive.

Diversification

Diversification is important to reduce risk and make the portfolio more manageable. Don't keep all your eggs in the same basket. You should own different types of assets. But even if you go for an aggressive 100% stock portfolio, you need to be very diverse in the stocks you hold. You should own many different industries, companies' sizes, locations, business models, etc. If you are properly diversified, one investment mistake will not wipe you out. Start with companies or sectors that interest you the most, and then go to the next industry or sector you find interesting.

Of course, you don't always need interest or prior knowledge of an industry to invest in.

It just makes the process more enjoyable. Certainly, if you notice a booming sector that is making considerable returns, and even if you have no real knowledge or interest in that sector, don't be afraid to study this investment opportunity to try and understand if you would like to add it to your portfolio.

Dividend Reinvestment

Another tip you might like to incorporate into your portfolio is investing in some dividend stocks. Apart from the diversification you get by adding yet another type of stock (in our case, it would be invested through an ETF or index fund), you also have the bonus of dividend payments every quarter or semi-annually. With this dividend payment, you can choose to do whatever you like with it. In my opinion, one of the best things the young investor can do with dividends is reinvest them to buy more shares. The benefit of this approach is the ease at which you can reinvest into that company or fund each time you receive a dividend.

On top of the ease of investment, you also benefit from a rather cheap form of investing as the brokerage firm won't charge a commission or trade fee, as the investment is automatic. In many cases, brokerage firms won't allow you to buy fractional shares, but when you reinvest dividends, you can get fractions of shares by using this strategy. This would also be considered a form of dollar-cost averaging, as you regularly invest a small amount of capital (the dividend) in the market—ensuring you don't go all-in at the wrong time.

Of course, there will be times when taking the dividend in cash might be better suited. If you notice the company is performing poorly, you might like to take the dividend as cash and invest elsewhere (this shouldn't be a problem with a dividend fund). If you wanted more diversification, you could take the dividend and reinvest it into another stock or fund. Also, for those people who are getting nearer to retirement, the cash coming into their bank will be a better option, rather than risking more by reinvesting the dividends.

Passive Stock Market Investing

In the final section of this chapter, we will highlight the key principles a young investor should understand to make money in the stock market passively. If we provide examples of accounts or investment options for you, please understand they are only examples of what is available to a teenage investor. Take what you learn from this chapter and throughout the book, and use this as your starting point. If you have found a particular account or investment option appealing, research the option further before investing.

Before we discuss what investment options might be best suited to the young investor, we need to mention that without a custodial account (or underaged investment account in the country you live in), you won't be able to get started on your investment journey. Until you turn 18 or 21—depending on your state—you can then invest fully without restriction. So if teenage investing interests you, discuss this with a parent or guardian and follow the steps to opening your first account.

Retirement accounts

As I said before, being smart about taxes will pay off in the long run. Roth IRAs are probably the best account to optimize taxes, especially when you have a lot of time. The younger you are, the more you can benefit from the compounding effect of your money working inside the account, plus the bonus of the money being tax-free when you retire is amazing. In addition to the tax advantages, you can still withdraw the money you contributed without penalty from the Roth IRA. So this can also help you with a down payment of a house, for example, long before you retire. Then you keep the profits you made from investing in the Roth IRA account and allow it to grow over time.

You can use other accounts for investing that are more for the short or medium term. But a Roth IRA should be high on your list of potential accounts. It might also help convince your parents to open a custodial account for you, as it shows some serious commitment to preparing for the future.

One thing to remember here, however, is the majority of the money in the Roth IRA can only be withdrawn after retirement (59 ½ years of age). So if you are looking to invest now, intending to have lots of money by the time you turn 40, you also need to have more capital to invest in your account that is not contributed to your Roth IRA. This means you simply invest money in assets without the tax protective layer of the Roth IRA. But you can withdraw and use this invested money whenever and however you like. Identify how much you would like to contribute to your retirement each year and use the remaining cash to invest in the near future.

Index funds

Index funds are a great place to start for beginner investors. They provide excellent diversification. They have good average returns over the long term and require very little knowledge to get started. The low fees are yet another bonus, as they are not eating up gains nor slowing down the compounding effect. Here is what to look for in a good index fund:

- High diversification across sectors (no sector should make up more than 30%–40% of the total).
- Low fees (also called expense ratio): ideally below 0.2.
- High trading volume/high liquidity. Popular indexes like the S&P 500 are a good place to start looking.
- No investment minimums.

To help you find what may be your first index fund investment, let's quickly revisit a strong potential candidate.

Total U.S. stock market funds

These index funds are broad and diverse across the U.S. stock market. The funds will purchase a basket of stocks with the hope of matching a specific equity index. Examples of the indexes that the funds try to replicate are the Russell 2000, the S&P 500, and the Wilshire 5000 Total Market Index. As the name suggests, the indexes themselves track a large number of companies, 2,000, 500, and 5,000, respectively.

With this excellent diversification, the funds can provide you with relatively low risk and have shown excellent returns over the past century. They are the passive investor's dream as they are low cost, highly diverse, and require little to no work on the part of the investor.

So if you are looking for a place to invest today, then perhaps they might be the best option for teen investors. Remember, it's best not to try and time the market. Instead, use a dollar-cost averaging approach and constantly invest in the market over time. Once you become more comfortable with investing and have gained more experience with the process, then maybe you might like to try some other index funds that require a little more knowledge to invest in successfully.

ETFs

If you pick an index fund, I recommend focusing on a very diverse option. If you want to be more specific, you can focus on one sector or industry easily using an ETF. Rather than simply picking a "tech" index fund like the Nasdaq Composite, you can pick an ETF that more specifically tracks software stocks, electronic chip makers, renewable energy or social media—the difference being the larger list of options available through ETFs. So while some ETFs are basically index funds in disguise, most are a lot less diversified and focus on a narrower section of the market.

There are also ETFs that track indexes and broader markets. But if you have a particular interest or specific market in mind that you feel you already have good knowledge of, then look for an ETF in that sector or industry. Also, if you are constructing your portfolio and notice it is lacking in a particular area—perhaps it is extremely conservative, and you have chosen assets that are very safe and secure, but you now have low returns projected for the future—maybe you then want to add a small amount of risk into the portfolio. With an ETF, you have many different options to do so. You could add an ETF that tracks growth funds, foreign stocks, IPO stocks or any high risk asset you might like.

The same can be said if you notice your portfolio is lacking elsewhere. Whether it is missing bonds, it's not very diverse, missing a high performing sector, too high risk, too low risk, too domestic or too foreign, you can fill that gap using exchange-traded funds. Let's round out this section by looking at a popular ETF option that can give you an example of what is out there and where you can begin looking for one that suits you.

A Developed Economy Foreign ETF

The idea of this ETF is to give you exposure to a foreign market while also reducing risk by investing in developed countries. Developed countries include places like the United Kingdom, some European countries, Japan, Australia, Canada and China. These countries will be similar to the United States regarding volatility and risk, especially when you are using funds to invest in the markets. Rather than investing large amounts in developing markets, maybe you would like to offset the risk by placing more emphasis on an ETF that contains developed economies.

This way, your portfolio is now diversified outside of the U.S., while also taking on similar risk to a fund that tracks American stock. Of course, you can still run into problems associated with these funds. If a country in the fund engages in war, or a government becomes corrupt or introduces harsh regulations on the industry the fund holds, it can begin to hurt your bottom line. Also, be aware of currency issues, which can cripple your investment if things go wrong.

CONCLUSION

"Nothing in the world is worth having or worth doing unless it means effort, pain, difficulty . I have never in my life envied a human being who led an easy life. I have envied a great many people who led difficult lives and led them well."

Theodore Roosevelt

I truly believe if you can dream it, you can achieve it. Of course, I'm not naive to the fact that becoming a CEO or creating a million-dollar business is as easy as dreaming it into reality. I mean if you want something so bad in life and are willing to work consistently for years, you can achieve almost anything. True, you might not be able to run a mile in under 4 minutes or run the 100-meter dash in under 10 seconds. But the only difference between you and Elon Musk, apart from his 155 IQ, (Yadav, A. K. (2022, January 17)) is his willingness to work until the job is finished.

I'm certainly not one of the people who work every waking hour of the day. I started this investing journey in the first place to find more freedom, so why box yourself into a routine that leaves no room for fun? But the reality is to achieve all your life goals; you need to be willing to work extremely hard and sacrifice.

I know everyone wants the path of least resistance, and if you have an easier option on your journey, take it. But the path to successful investing is not as simple as putting $100 a month in an index fund.

First, we need to work a part-time job or create a side hustle and save enough each month to invest. We then need to educate ourselves constantly to get the edge on other investors. We also need to work hard to develop a winning strategy and a portfolio designed for success. A strong work ethic may not have been something you were born with, but it is something you can develop. Don't panic if you don't see much progress over the first few years or even decades. I know that might sound crazy, but to truly create wealth in the stock market, you either need a lot of skill, luck or a lot of time.

The idea of passive investing is to let the market rise over time, watching your investments grow until eventually, you have enough money to retire early. Remember, though, don't forget to live your life, make time and use some of your money to create lasting memories with friends and family. You can still go on a few holidays throughout your teenage years and invest successfully. Just don't buy a Starbucks or McDonald's every day and waste a lot of your hard-earned income.

This book is the first step on your investing journey; don't be afraid to reread the book if you have found any section complicated, and feel welcome to email admin@younginvestorbob with any questions you may have. For those of you excited about the thoughts of actively investing, keep an eye out for our second book in the Stock Market Investing For Teens series. In this part of the series, we will dive deeper again into the technical nature of active stock market investing and cover another range of topics designed to make you a more profitable investor.

REVIEWS

Dear Reader,

Thank you for taking the time to read my book. As the author, I poured my heart and soul into every page, and it was not an easy journey. There were times when I felt like giving up, but my passion for writing and my desire to share this story with others kept me going.

As you may know, reviews are crucial for authors. They not only provide valuable feedback but also help us to reach more readers. Your review can make a significant impact on the success of my book, and it would mean the world to me if you could take a few moments to share your thoughts.

Your review could be the one that encourages someone else to pick up the book and read it. Your words could inspire someone to take action, make a change, or see the world in a different way.

Your review could help me to grow as a writer and reach even more readers. I want you to know that I will read every single review personally. Your feedback is valuable to me, and I appreciate your support. Thank you for taking the time to read my book; I hope it helped you improve your life somehow.

Please scan the QR code below to leave a review of my book on Amazon.

Sincerely,

Robert Reid

admin@younginvestorbob.com

CONCLUSION

SCAN ME

DISCLAIMER

The Content is for informational purposes only, you should not construe any such information or other material as legal, tax, investment, financial, or other advice. Nothing contained in our book constitutes a solicitation, recommendation, endorsement, or offer by The Young Investor or any third party service provider to buy or sell any securities or other financial instruments in this or in any other jurisdiction in which such solicitation or offer would be unlawful under the securities laws of such jurisdiction.

All Content in this book is information of a general nature and does not address the circumstances of any particular individual or entity. Nothing in this book constitutes professional and/or financial advice, nor does any information in the book constitute a comprehensive or complete statement of the matters discussed or the law relating thereto. The Young Investor is not a fiduciary by virtue of any person's use of or access in this book or Content. You alone assume the sole responsibility of evaluating the merits and risks associated with the use of any information or other Content in this book before making any decisions based on such information or other Content. In exchange for purchasing this book, you agree not to hold The Young Investor, its affiliates or any third party service provider liable for any possible claim for damages arising from any decision you make based on information or other Content made available to you through the book.

BIBLIOGRAPHY

Chen, J. (2021, May 19). What is passive investing? Investopedia. Retrieved May 7, 2022, from https://www.investopedia.com/terms/p/passiveinvesting.asp

Blystone, D. (2021, August 24). Who is Elon Musk? Investopedia. Retrieved April 20, 2022, fromhttps://www.investopedia.com/articles/personal-finance/061015/how-elon-musk-became-elon-musk.asp

Loredo, A. (2022, January 3). Daily routine examples for financial success. Clever Girl Finance. Retrieved April 22, 2022, from https://www.clevergirlfinance.com/blog/daily-routine-examples/

Lee, N. L. (2020, November 10). Insider. Insider. Retrieved March 8, 2022, from https://www.businessinsider.com/warren-buffett-modest-home-bought-31500-looks-2017-6?r=US&IR=T

O'Neill, A. (2022, February 2). United States - life expectancy of men. Statista. Retrieved April 22, 2022, from https://www.statista.com/statistics/263731/life-expectancy-of-men-in-the-united-states/

Lake, R. (2022, March 28). Retire by 40? here's how to do it. Investopedia. Retrieved April 22, 2022, from https://www.investopedia.com/retire-by-40-here-s-how-to-do-it-4770878

Lyck, M. (2020, December 28). Why 80% of day traders lose money. Medium. Retrieved April 22, 2022, from https://marklyck.medium.com/why-80-of-day-traders-lose-money-78d51b10fe25

Chakrabarti, R. (2017, June 14). #9 out of 10 start-ups fail. here's why! Entrepreneur. Retrieved May 14, 2022, from https://www.entrepreneur.com/article/295798

Luthi, B. (2021, November 4). Rule of thumb for average stock market return. The Balance. Retrieved May 8, 2022, from https://www.thebalance.com/rule-of-thumb-for-average-stock-market-return-5115017#:~:text=The%20stock%20market%20has%20re-turned,is%20only%20a%20starting%20place

Topic no. 409 capital gains and losses. Internal Revenue Service. (2022, February 3). Retrieved April 8, 2022, from https://www.irs.gov/taxtopics/tc409

Chen, J. (2021, May 19). What is passive investing? Investopedia. Retrieved April 9, 2022, from https://www.investopedia.com/terms/p/passiveinvesting.asp

Bloomberg. (n.d.). Bloomberg.com. Retrieved April 9, 2022, from https://www.bloomberg.com/news/articles/2021-11-24/active-v-passive-why-it-s-not-that-simple-anymore-quicktake

The active vs. passive debate. S&P Global. (2020, January 13). Retrieved April 9, 2022, from https://www.spglobal.com/en/research-insights/articles/the-active-vs-passive-debate

Malkiel, B. G. (2003). A random walk down wall street. W.W. Norton & Company

O'Connell, B. (2021, December 8). Investing basics: What is a portfolio? Forbes. Retrieved April 29, 2022, from https://www.forbes.com/advisor/investing/portfolio/

Jackson, A.-L. (2021, July 30). What is sector rotation? Forbes. Retrieved April 29, 2022, from https://www.forbes.com/advisor/investing/what-is-sector-rotation/

Tepper, T. (2021, May 12). The historical performance of stocks and Bonds. Forbes. Retrieved May 8, 2022, from https://www.forbes.com/advisor/investing/stock-and-bond-returns/

Boyer Posted 1 year ago, C. (2021, April 11). How often should you check your investments? Wealthify.com. Retrieved April 11, 2022, from https://www.wealthify.com/blog/how-often-should-you-check-your-investments

Beattie, A. (2022, March 14). The birth of stock exchanges. Investopedia. Retrieved April 11, 2022, from https://www.investopedia.com/articles/07/stock-exchange-history.asp

Hwang, I. (2022, March 7). A brief history of the stock market. SoFi. Retrieved April 11, 2022, from https://www.sofi.com/learn/content/history-of-the-stock-market/

FRANK, ADAM (n.d.). Custodial accounts. J.P. Morgan. Retrieved April 11, 2022, from https://www.jpmorgan.com/wealth-management/wealth-partners/insights/custodial-accounts

Segal, T. (2021, December 7). When does a person need a custodial account? Investopedia. Retrieved April 11, 2022, from https://www.investopedia.com/terms/c/custodialaccount.asp

Roth IRA withdrawal rules. Schwab Brokerage. (n.d.). Retrieved April 12, 2022, from https://www.schwab.com/ira/roth-ira/withdrawal-rules

Lake, R. (2022, March 30). What is the average stock market return? SoFi. Retrieved April 12, 2022, from https://www.sofi.com/learn/content/average-stock-market-return/

Hassine, M. (2016). Analysing active & passive fund performance - lyxor ETF. Retrieved April 12, 2022, from https://www.lyxoretf.de/pdfDocuments/Lyxor%20ETF%20Active%20vs%20Passive%202019%20INTERACT-FINAL-VERSION.PDF6-da15f47be17be6ac8ee5cdc7a0c40c6.pdf

Johnston, M. (2022, February 8). Top S&P 500 index funds. Investopedia. Retrieved April 12, 2022, from https://www.investopedia.com/articles/markets/101415/4-best-sp-500-index-funds.asp

Chang, E. (2019, July 26). Why you should consider small-cap index funds - US news money. Why You Should Consider Small-Cap Index FundsEle. Retrieved April 30, 2022, from https://money.usnews.com/investing/funds/articles/why-you-should-consider-small-cap-index-funds

Chang, E. (2019, July 26). Why you should consider small-cap index funds - US news money. Why You Should Consider Small-Cap Index FundsEle. Retrieved April 30, 2022, from https://money.usnews.com/investing/funds/articles/why-you-should-consider-small-cap-index-funds

U.S. Bureau of Labor Statistics. (2016, April 28). Business establishment age. U.S. Bureau of Labor Statistics. Retrieved April 30, 2022, from https://www.bls.gov/bdm/entrepreneurship/entrepreneurship.htm

Kenny, T. (2022, March 1). The benefits and risks of Bond Index Funds. The Balance. Retrieved April 30, 2022, from https://www.thebalance.com/the-benefits-and-risks-of-bond-index-funds-416976

Blokhin, A. (2022, April 25). The 4 best international equity index mutual funds. Investopedia. Retrieved April 30, 2022, from https://www.investopedia.com/articles/investing/011916/4-best-international-equity-index-mutual-funds.asp

Knueven, L. (2021, June 14). The average stock market return over the past 10 years. Business Insider. Retrieved April 30, 2022, from https://www.businessinsider.com/personal-finance/average-stock-market-return?r=US&IR=T

Davis, C. (2022, March 16). Index fund vs. ETF: What's the difference? NerdWallet. Retrieved May 10, 2022, from https://www.nerdwallet.com/article/investing/etf-vs-index-fund-compare#:~:text=What's%20the%20difference%20between%20an,end%20of%20the%20trading%20day

Hayes, A. (2022, February 8). What is a growth stock? Investopedia. Retrieved May 2, 2022, from https://www.investopedia.com/terms/g/growthstock.asp

What are the different types of etfs and how do they work? Merrill Edge. (n.d.). Retrieved

April 12, 2022, from https://www.merrilledge.com/article/getting-to-know-exchange-traded-funds

Hicks, C. (2021, February 1). ETF vs. Index Fund: The difference and which to use ... ETF vs. Index Fund: The Difference and Which to Use. Retrieved April 12, 2022, from https://money.usnews.com/investing/investing-101/articles/etf-vs-index-fund-the-difference-and-which-to-use

Graham, B. (2003). The Intelligent Investor. HarperBusiness.

Segal, T. (2022, February 9). The Pros and cons of etfs. Investopedia. Retrieved May 2, 2022, from https://www.investopedia.com/articles/exchangetradedfunds/11/advantages-disadvantages-etfs.asp

Segal, T. (2022, February 9). The Pros and cons of etfs. Investopedia. Retrieved May 2, 2022, from https://www.investopedia.com/articles/exchangetradedfunds/11/advantages-disadvantages-etfs.asp

Davis, A. (2018, December 18). *At one point, Amazon lost more than 90% of its value. but long-term investors still got rich.* CNBC. Retrieved May 13, 2022, from https://www.cnbc.com/2018/12/18/dotcom-bubble-amazon-stock-lost-more-than-90percent-long-term-investors-still-got-rich.html

Snelling, D. (2020, November 3). Investment funds – 12 pros and cons of active and passive funds. Charlton House. Retrieved May 2, 2022, from https://charltonhousewealthman-agement.hk/investment-funds-12-pros-and-cons-of-active-and-passive-funds/

Hayes, A. (2022, March 21). Dollar-cost averaging (DCA). Investopedia. Retrieved May 3, 2022, from https://www.investopedia.com/terms/d/dollarcostaverag-ing.asp#:~:text=Dollar%2Dcost%20averaging%20does%20 improve,will%2C%20eventually%2C%20always%20rise

Ganatra, M. (2022, March 29). What is a robo-advisor and how does it work? Forbes. Retrieved May 6, 2022, from https://www.forbes.com/advisor/in/investing/what-is-a-robo-advisor-and-how-does-it-work/

Henricks, M. (2022, February 9). Robo advisor fees: How much it costs. SmartAsset. Retrieved May 6, 2022, from https://smartasset.com/investing/robo-advisor-fees#:~:text=The%20biggest%20part%20of%20what, %241%2C000%20to%20%242%2C000%20each%20year

Yadav, A. K. (2022, January 17). *What is Elon Musk's IQ and why is he a genius?* TecValue. Retrieved May 13, 2022, from https://tecvalue.com/what-is-elon-musk-iq/

Made in the USA
Coppell, TX
05 November 2023

23864558R00069